WHITEHAVEN

REBIRTH OF A SOUTHERN MANSION

WHITEHAVEN
WELCOME TO
KENTUCKY

WHITEHAVEN

REBIRTH OF A SOUTHERN MANSION

by RICHARD HOLLAND

McClanahan
Publishing House

Library of Congress Catalog Card Number: 87-060373
International Standard Book Number: 0-913383-07-4 $21.95

Cover photograph: Whitehaven, Paducah, Kentucky

Cover photograph by Dave Stanley
Book layout and design by James Asher
Cover design by James Asher

Manufactured in the United States of America
Printed by Arcata Graphics, Kingsport, Tennessee

All book order correspondence should be addressed to:
McClanahan Publishing House, Incorporated
P.O. Box 100
Kuttawa, Kentucky 42055
Tel: 502 388 9388
1 800 544 6959 (outside Kentucky)

Dedication

May, 1988, marked the seventh anniversary of the Whitehaven project. In my mind, the project started in May, 1981, with the visit to Paducah of Governor John Y. Brown and Secretary Frank Metts. This visit sparked the first interest by the state in restoring Whitehaven.

In those seven years, we have lost several good friends to Whitehaven. Judge Raymond Schultz, who provided much needed support for the project when it was first proposed; Jack Paxton, who utilized his position as editor of the *Paducah Sun* to champion the project and to explain eloquently why the house had to be saved; Marian Widener, an original member of the Whitehaven Association Board, who brought enthusiasm and dedication to the project; and Richard Pair, who provided much of the sensitive design work for the planning on how to restore Whitehaven. This book is dedicated to these fine people. They are missed.

RICHARD HOLLAND
December, 1988

Acknowledgements _____

For this book, I had over 2000 photographs to choose from for inclusion. I would like to thank the many sources that provided some of the materials included in the book, such as:

Mary Shelton Moseley, for the Smith family photographs that belonged to her mother Elizabeth Smith Shelton.

Pat Kerr, Whitehaven restoration architect, for the photographs taken by Dana Curtis that were used in the restoration planning process.

Kentucky Department of Transportation, for photographs of the grand opening ceremony.

Bill Black, Jr., Whitehaven restoration contractor, for his many photographs documenting the Whitehaven restoration process.

Ann Brown, for copies of the Whitehaven stencil patterns.

Kentucky Heritage Council, for the photographs taken in 1979 by a survey team that recorded Whitehaven as a historic site.

Dottie Barkley, for photographs taken in 1968 by her father David Barkley of the interior of the house when Elizabeth Smith Shelton lived there.

Paducah Sun, for several photographs taken during the restoration process and the photograph of Jack Paxton.

Kit Wesler, with the Murray State University Archaeology Program, for photographs of the archaeological dig at Whitehaven.

Marty Godbey, for use of her photographs on page 2 and on page 70.

Tom Clauser, of Curtis & Mays Studio, Paducah, Ky. for Christmas at Whitehaven photos.

Many people provided important information to me concerning the history of Whitehaven. I was able to meet twice with Elizabeth Smith Shelton, who graciously answered many of my questions about the house and her family. Two of my favorite people in the world, Toots DuBois Smith and Gerry Krueger Smith, shared with me many of their memories of life at "Bide-A-Wee."

Two of architect A.L. Lassiter's descendants, Inez Hardin and Jane Farr McElya, provided me with information about Mr. Lassiter and the Atkins family. Inez Hardin, who remembers as a child riding in a pony cart to visit the Atkins family at Whitehaven, provided me with the earliest photograph of the house, taken in 1903 by A.L. Lassiter.

Assisting me with presenting an accurate record of the restoration process were Pat Kerr and Bill Black, Jr. who read and corrected all of the copy. My good friends Jane Bright and Mary Dyer also read the copy and offered suggestions and comments.

A special word of appreciation to my family, who have constantly encouraged me with this and all my endeavors.

Table of Contents

Introduction

Even as a child, Whitehaven always fascinated me. I can distinctly remember riding along Lone Oak Road and pressing my nose up to the car window, watching for the beautiful white house in the distance.

When I returned to Paducah in 1979 to begin my career as a historic preservationist, this house continued to fascinate me. Of course by then, the house was a rotting shell of its former grandeur. Whenever I

WHITEHAVEN - 1945

drove by, I had a sick feeling in my stomach. I resisted all impulses to go up and walk through the house, for the same basic reasons that I avoided going to funerals and to the dentist.

I first walked into Whitehaven on a sunny warm day in April, 1981. The very first event had taken place that would eventually lead to the restoration of the house and WPSD-TV wanted to do a story. Specifically, they wanted to know if the house could be saved.

I went out to the house early and slowly walked through it. Standing in the front hallway, my first impression was one of tremendous light and airiness, primarily because the house no longer had doors and windows. I felt that the house was almost no longer a manmade object, but with the overgrown vegetation and the atmosphere of rot and decay, had reverted to being a part of nature. And, I will always remember the buzz of hundreds of bees over my head.

But even with the rotting floors, missing windows, and cracked plaster, I recognized that the house still had beauty and proportion, a sense of grandeur that could not be destroyed. I thought, "We have to save this house."

On that warm afternoon, I stood on the front porch at Whitehaven, smiled at the television camera, hid my own doubts, and told the world, "Of course this house can be saved. And, we will find a way to do it!"

It was in the following months that what I call the "miracle of Whitehaven" took place. Officially, the Department of Transportation for the state of Kentucky purchased the property and restored it as a Tourist Welcome Center and rest area for Interstate 24. Unofficially, it took the tremendous effort of hundreds of dedicated people to preserve the house and bring it back to life. For all of us involved, I think we innately knew how important this project was and that we had to give our very best to it. Personally, I knew that the restoration of Whitehaven might be the most important project of my life. I am grateful to have been a part of it all.

History of Whitehaven

Whitehaven has always been more than a building of brick and plaster. This majestic landmark has been cherished by the people of Paducah and the surrounding area. The grand mansion, once destined to be destroyed, has now been restored for a new and exciting history (or future) as the Whitehaven Tourist Welcome Center.

Whitehaven possesses great architectural and historical significance. What began as a simple farmhouse evolved into one of the finest Classical Revival residential structures in Kentucky.

The main portion of the house was built by Edward L. Anderson, who came to Paducah with his family in 1850. A member of the business partnership of Anderson and Brandon, Mr. Anderson was a tobacco dealer and landowner. Wanting his family to live in the country, Mr. Anderson in 1859 bought a 62 acre plot of land for $4500 three miles from Paducah on the Paducah and Lovelaceville Gravel Road. Under his direction, a two story brick house was constructed.

The bricks were handmade and baked on the property. Construction continued on the house from 1859 to 1865, with work being disturbed by events of the Civil War. Family members have passed down stories of Union soldiers raiding the house.

The home was a simple two story farmhouse with a central doorway, wood lintels above the windows, and a front porch. The kitchen was in a separate building behind the main house.

In 1872, Mr. Anderson died and the land with the house on it went to his daughter, Mary Anderson. The house remained in the Anderson family until 1903 when it was sold to Ed L. Atkins, the cashier at the American German Bank. The McCracken County Deed Books reveal that the property was conveyed to Ed Atkins by Norton B. Anderson on April 7, 1903 for $4,000. Atkins

Above: This is the earliest photograph of the Smith family at Bide-A-Wee, taken around 1910 during a birthday party for the eldest daughter, Elizabeth. A postcard made from this photograph had the inscription "BIDE-A-WEE SUMMER HOME OF MAYOR J. P. SMITH PADUCAH, KENTUCKY." Note that the attic dormer windows and carport had not yet been added. Left: The Smith's three oldest children were, from left to right, Elizabeth (Bodgie), Augustus (Gus), and James R. (Jim). The Smiths had three more children, Mary Orr, Charles, and Richard, the only child actually born at Bide-A-Wee.

commissioned his good friend A. L. Lassiter to do a complete remodelling of the house. Lassiter had recently proved his adeptness with working in the Classical Revival style with his outstanding design for the Carnegie Library in downtown Paducah. Lassiter's design for the Anderson house transformed it into one of the most beautiful and up-to-date houses in Western Kentucky. Whitehaven was recognized then, as it is today, as one of the great landmarks of the area.

The most startling change Lassiter made to the house was the addition of a grandiose Corinthian columned front portico. The eight massive columns were wood

Above: Paducah architect, A. L. Lassiter, whose sensitive design work transformed a farmhouse into a mansion worthy of the name, Whitehaven.

Left: The addition of the Corinthian-columned front portico added a sense of grandeur and majesty to the house. This photograph, taken by the Sacra Studio of Paducah, shows the front portico during the early occupancy of the house by the Smith family.

with plaster capitals. A new classical front doorway was added with flat Corinthian-topped pilasters and bevelled glass windows. A balcony was installed above the entranceway.

Stained and bevelled glass were used extensively in the house. The most elaborate window was installed above the staircase landing with the date "1903" placed in it. A mantel with the words "Whitehaven" carved into it was assembled in one of the front parlors. Elaborate plaster ceilings graced each of the downstairs rooms and

the front hallway. Crown molding was added to the Victorian woodwork above the double pocket doors in each of the two front rooms downstairs. Colored stenciling was applied in most of the rooms.

A new grand staircase was built in the front hallway, with decoratively carved spindles and bannisters. The area between the main house and the kitchen was enclosed and converted into a butler's pantry. The exterior of the house was painted white for the first time and Mr. Atkins named his new home Whitehaven, a title appropriate to its new grandeur and elegance.

The Atkins family was only able to enjoy their home for a very few years. Descendants of architect A.L. Lassiter remember that Mr. Atkins remodelled Whitehaven because of his great love for his wife Grace. Mrs. Atkins died soon after the family moved into the house and Mr. Atkins lost all interest in the house. He moved with his two daughters to Oklahoma and put the house up for sale.

On April 21, 1908, James P. Smith, the mayor of Paducah (1908-1912) purchased the house from Edward L. Atkins of Enid, Oklahoma, for $7000 cash in hand. Before moving to Whitehaven, the Smiths lived at Fifth and Washington Streets. Mr. Smith was a partner in a wholesale grocery business with his father, James R. Smith, and had extensive real estate holdings.

Smith family members relate that prior to moving out to the country, Mr. Smith would arrive home from work and find the house full of children. One day he said to his wife, "Nell, we're moving to the country to get away from the kids and the dust." The new house was apparently used by the Smiths as a summer house while Mr. Smith served as mayor but became a fulltime home by 1912.

Since Mrs. Smith was Scottish, she renamed the house "Bide-A-Wee" which is Scotch for "Come rest a while." The new name was inscribed in the leaded glass over the front doorway.

The Smiths made many changes to the house.

Opposite page:
Above left: Family and a servant pose on the front porch of the house.
Bottom left: The Smith's second son Gus and his nurse Miss Dock. Elizabeth sits in the background.
Bottom right: Gus and Miss Dock play in a tulip garden on the grounds.

Below: The Smith children frolic in an iris garden on a spring day at Bide-A-Wee.

Marshall Fields of Chicago was hired to do the interior decorating. The firm added damask draperies to the windows and to the sliding door openings between the rooms. Silk wallpaper was added to an upstairs bedroom. Wallpaper covered the other walls, including the 1903 stenciling. The Smiths built additional bedrooms onto the rear of the house for their six children, and they changed the attic into a playroom. The playroom had stenciling in an Oriental motiff of pagodas and willow trees, a massive square piano, and double dormer windows. At Christmas time, the playroom had a Christmas tree for each child lit with real candles.

The Smiths also installed a large closet in the master bedroom that was always referred to as "Mrs. Smith's closet." Other built-in closets were added to the front bedrooms. The family also added a pair of benches in the front hallway, bookshelves with bevelled glass

Above: The Smith children with their pony Uncle Sam.
Right: Bide-A-Wee seen from the end of the long sidewalk that led from the house down to Lone Oak Road. Carefully clipped hedge lined both sides of the sidewalk. Much of the front yard would later be taken for the expansion of Lone Oak Road.

doors in the library, large built-in mirrors in the upstairs hallway and the back hallway, and a family breakfast room. A carport was built to one side of the dwelling as well as a side entrance and back staircase to the east side of the house.

Mr. Smith was very concerned about the safety of his family and had a storm shelter built in the back yard. Whenever threatening weather occurred, the family

Some of the interior rooms at Bide-A-Wee as they appeared on May 19, 1968. Elizabeth Smith Shelton was planning to move that year to another house and asked family friend David Barkley to photograph the house for her. These photographs remain the best record of the appearance of the house while the Smith family lived there, and were a great assistance during the restoration process.

Below left: A writing desk in the parlor is surrounded with beloved family photographs and portraits.

Above left: A buffet and dining table in the family breakfast room, directly behind the main staircase.

Above: An upstairs bedroom; decorated in Elizabeth Shelton's favorite color of blue.

Two early means of transportation for the Smith family.

Below: The pony Uncle Sam and its wicker cart were used by the Smith children. One of the Smith family members remembered that the eldest son James R. taught the pony to rear up and dump the other children out of the cart.

Right: Mr. Smith used this beautiful carriage and his favorite horse Mac to travel to town to visit his wholesale grocery business. One of the Smith children sits inside the carriage in this photograph, taken on the drive at Bide-A-Wee.

would stay in the shelter until the danger passed. In later years, the storm shelter was to become a storage area for preserves and canned goods.

Bide-A-Wee was comprised of 22 rooms including a family breakfast room, parlor, library, music room, a playroom on the third floor, kitchen, formal dining room, butler's pantry, a cook's room, a downstairs lavatory, six upstairs bedrooms, three upstairs bathrooms, one dressing room, the upstairs sitting hallway, and a second-floor sunroom.

In order to care for the many rooms, the Smiths had servants. One couple lived in a small cottage on the grounds. The Smiths always employed a cook, maid, yardman and chauffeur. Each year the furnishings of the house were removed, room by room, and the floors cleaned with gasoline. Hired workers would scrub the floors with bricks covered by a heavy carpet-like material. One family member remembers the house always smelling of gasoline!

The original kitchen had a cast iron stove with an oven cover. At one time, the house had four refrigerators. The kitchen also had a table with a galvanized top and ladder-back chairs for the servants. Later the family bought an electric stove but really preferred food cooked on the cast iron stove because it tasted better.

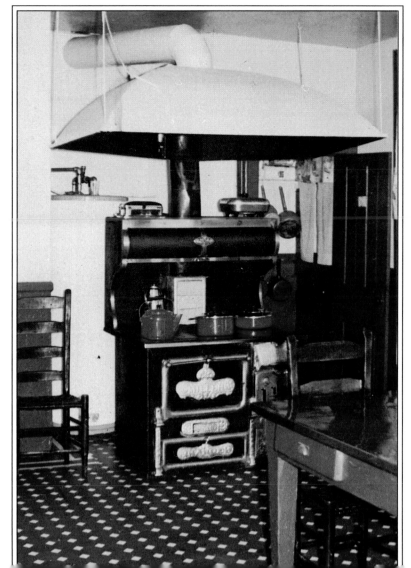

The kitchen in 1968, with the old cast-iron stove, galvanized-top table, and tile floor. This kitchen was especially busy during the 1937 flood, when the Smiths hosted over forty refugees. Mrs. Smith discovered that she had left her large coffee urn at the First Presbyterian Church and the cook had to make coffee in frying pans.

Two of the favorite sitting areas for the Smith family.

Right: In the winter, the family would gather in the comfortable upstairs hallway.

Below: On summer evenings, the family would sit on the front porch and enjoy the cool breeze provided by the overhead fan.

Right: The family's favorite photograph of Mr. and Mrs. Smith, showing "Big Jim" enjoying one of his cigars and "Mother Nell" surrounded by her much-loved hanging baskets.

FRONT PORCH

The front porch was a popular meeting place for family and friends during the summer months. It was furnished with all black wicker furniture, a round table with barrel back chairs, a tea cart, a desk, and chairs for the children. The columns were adorned with wire hanging baskets filled with ferns.

UPSTAIRS HALLWAY

During the winter months, the upstairs hall was the popular meeting place. It was furnished with a chaise lounge, a reading table, and two arm chairs. On either side of the hall mirror were placed two reclining styled chairs made of wood and upholstered in velvet.

Below: The front porch at Bide-A-Wee in the 1920s. In the background are three of the Smith sons, dressed in knickers, white shirts, and ties, with a pet dog. The concrete walk leads from the house to the road and mail box.

Right: The front porch of Bide-A-Wee always beckoned the Smith family as a cool oasis for sitting and conversation. Glimpsed on the porch are two of Mrs. Smith's favorite things, hanging baskets and bouquets of fresh flowers. The hanging baskets of ferns and flowers were used by Mrs. Smith to decorate the front balcony and columns. Mrs. Smith would also gather fresh flowers from the garden for arrangements in the house. This brass container holds a bouquet of white peonies, one of Mrs. Smith's favorite flowers.

CHRISTMAS AT BIDE-A-WEE

Christmas was a popular holiday to the Smith family. In front of the mirror in the back downstairs hallway sat a stuffed Santa Claus from Chicago's Marshall Fields. Mrs. Smith filled the Santa with pillows to make him look even more real. The columns to the side entrance were wrapped with satin ribbons. The stairway and every mantel were decorated, and the house glittered

Below: A photograph of Bide-A-Wee, taken in 1945 for a Christmas card for the Smiths. Over the years, there have been several changes to the house and grounds, including the replacement of earlier landscaping with evergreens, hollies, and hackberry trees. The area over the carport has also been enclosed for a bedroom.

The Smiths hosted a July wedding of their daughter Elizabeth to Russell Shelton. The wedding celebration took place on the front porch, which was elaborately decorated with greenery. Elizabeth Smith Shelton would later move back into Bide-A-Wee with her two children after the death of her husband in 1941.

Mr. and Mrs. Russell Lewis Shelton photographed on the portico at "Bide-a-Wee," the country home of the bride's parents, Mr. and Mrs. James Peterson Smith, immediately after the wedding ceremony at 5:00 the afternoon of Wednesday, July 22, which united two old and socially prominent Paducah families.

Paducah News-Democrat
July 26, 1925

*Elizabeth Shelton's daughter, Mary Orr
(Sudie), entertains a group of friends at her
13th birthday party. Attending were (from
left to right) Kate Rudy, Mildred Terrell,
Barbaranelle Paxton, Ann Katterjohn,
Margie Terrell, Judy Woodall, Sally Martin,
Sudie Shelton, Gretchen Oehlschlaeger.*

with white and silver trim. A Christmas tree in the library
was almost the height of the ceiling and the gifts literally
reached to the hallway. Charles, one of the sons, always
played the role of Santa Claus.

*Below: Sudie Shelton poses by her
grandmother's lily pond.*

THE GARDENS

Mrs. Smith and her daughter, Elizabeth Smith Shelton, were avid gardeners. They cared for a cutting garden in which they grew larkspur, church lilies, spring bulbs, zinnias, marigolds, chrysanthemums, oriental poppies, peonies, and many others. A nearby cistern (the current gazebo) was used to provide water for the family and flowers. The area above the cistern had a railing around it for pots and for preparing plants for friends. Mrs. Smith also provided flowers for the First Presbyterian Church. To the south of the cistern was a brick patio bordered with forsythia and hibiscus with a walkway to the property line. Next to this was a hedge with an iron gate. Behind the hedge was a lily pond with statuary. These gardens were very formal, and at one time were toured by members of the southern zone of the Garden Club of America.

Bide-A-Wee at its peak as the residence of the Smith family. The house was chosen as the backdrop for this special photograph taken in 1956 by the Paducah Sun-Democrat.

The Smiths lived many happy years at Bide-A-Wee until the last member of the family moved out in 1968.

Years of Decline 1968-1981

These never-before-published photographs record Bide-A-Wee at the midpoint of its decline. The house was photographed in May, 1979 by a survey team from the Kentucky Heritage Commission, the state historic preservation office. At this point, the house was being inhabited by a family of caretakers. Although the house was still structurally sound, signs of deterioration were evident, especially in the decay of the front portico and the early signs of collapse of the east wall.

Also contributing to the sense of decline was the appearance of the grounds. Old tires and hubcaps decorated the front yard, wringer washing machines and recliners stood on the front porch, a mattress leaned against the carport wall, and boxes of old clothing and junk were scattered throughout the inside of the house.

Stories abound about the family of caretakers who lived in the house during those years. Supposedly, the children in the family set up a hoop in the library

Years of neglect begin to take their toll on the house. This photo, taken in 1979, shows the deterioration of the front portico due to water damage. The neglected yard and the trash on the front porch also add to the sense of decline.

Above: In 1979, the east wall was showing the first signs of collapse.

Right top: Two years later, the east wall had collapsed, with the area of collapse concentrated on the wall behind the fireplace in the library.

Right bottom: The front of the house had also deteriorated into ruins. All of the windows and doors had been broken by vandals and water deterioration had rotted away the front portico. The west column and its plaster capital had collapsed into the front yard, shattering the capital into hundreds of pieces.

and turned the room into a basketball court. Other family members cooked over a charcoal grill in the dining room. A malnourished pony was kept tied up in the front yard until the local Humane Society intervened. Many people remember touring the house, for a fee of five dollars, and being offered for sale parts of the house such as door knobs and light fixtures. In a bizarre act of decorating, someone highlighted, with blue paint, the plaster ceilings in the hallway and music room.

After the caretaker's family moved out in 1979, the house drastically declined. It was stripped of all its finer detail, including the stained and bevelled glass windows, mantels, the double benches from the front hallway, balcony railings and many of the doors. Vandals

Above left: The original bevelled glass window reading WHITEHAVEN was still in place in 1979. By 1981, it was missing, along with the other decorative glass in the house.

Above right: Old tires and washing machines rest on a front porch where wicker furniture and ferns once stood.

Left and right: Destruction and decay surrounded the once stately mansion.

Beautiful architectural details remain,
despite vandalism and decay.

Above: While vandals have removed the
bevelled glass from the front doorway, the
plaster and wood pilasters survive to
provide grace to the entrance. The remains
of the west column, rescued from the front
yard, lay on the front porch.

Right: Sadly in need of a coat of paint, one
of the plaster capitals for the two-story
porch pilasters also survives.

broke all the remaining windows, ripped down sections of plaster walls, and kicked in many of the spindles on the staircase. Water damage gradually rotted ceilings, floors and the front portico. For many people of Paducah and, of western Kentucky, the house took on a ghostly, abandoned appearance reminiscent of a scene out of a William Faulkner novel.

Page 34: The dining room before restoration, looking toward the butler's pantry, the door on the right to the family breakfast room.

Insert: The same room after restoration and conversion into the state tourist information room.

Above: After years of clogged gutters, water damage has rotted away much of the front architrave of the portico.

Page 35: The music room, looking toward the library, before restoration. The finer details of the room, such as the woodwork and the plaster cornice molding, remain. In the library, the original library book shelves are visible.

Insert: The music room and library after restoration.

Below: One of the walls in the dining room, with the doorway leading to the front hall. Peeling wallpaper reveals the original grapevine stencil, designed to compliment the vine pattern in the plaster molding.

Spring of 1981

It will always be my contention that the rescue and restoration of Whitehaven was a miracle. All the pieces fell into place in the spring of 1981.

For years, the Smith family had been trying to find a buyer for the property. One obstacle to selling the property was the family's intention of grouping the entire 32 acre parcel as a single unit, without dividing it into smaller lots.

In April, 1981, the Paducah Junior College Board of Trustees announced that it had purchased the 32 acres as land for future expansion of the college. Rumors began circulating about the immediate demolition of the Smith mansion. The board assured the public that it had no pending plans to demolish the house and would entertain proposals to save it. At the same time, the college made clear its decision that it was not in a position to restore the house for use as part of the campus.

The second step in the road to rescue came about in May, 1981, when Governor John Y. Brown and his cabinet visited Paducah where they conducted a Town Hall meeting at city hall. At this gathering, Governor Brown announced that a welcome center would be built off Interstate 24, and that several sites were under consideration. An earlier plan to build the welcome center near the Ohio River had been cancelled by the Brown administration because of excessive costs. However, funds in the amount of 3 million dollars had been specifically allocated by the Federal Department of Transportation for the construction of this welcome center.

Immediately following the Town Hall meeting, a reception for Governor Brown and his cabinet was given by Paducah-McCracken County Growth, Inc. at the home of Growth's president, Allan Rhodes. Attending the reception was Secretary of Transportation for Kentucky, Frank Metts. Several local citizens cornered Secretary Metts and explained to him the potential in restoring the Smith house as the site of the new tourist welcome center on I-24 as opposed to building new facilities.

Being an active preservationist in Louisville himself, Metts immediately recognized the potential of this new idea. Arrangements were quickly made and he visited the site and visualized the house as it would be restored. He then requested background information about the house, which was provided by local contacts Pat Kerr and Carroll Ladt.

A final decision was made late Monday, June 9, 1981, when Secretary Metts received reports from engineers that ramp access for north-south traffic to the site would be no problem. The state would accept the project!

Right: Broken glass and plaster litter the floor of the upstairs hallway. The French doors leading to the front balcony remain, but the pair of stained glass windows are gone. Visible also are two of the capitals of the portico columns.

Public Reaction

There was strong public reaction to the state's announcement, both positive and negative. Some project proponents hailed it as an innovative means to provide the state with a beautiful and unique welcome center. Other supporters expressed relief that a concrete plan had been found to save the Smith house.

Project opponents, on the other hand, while not against saving the house, questioned the feasibility of using the site as a tourist information center. They expressed strong concern about the access roads to the center from the interstate and the lack of visibility of the center. They strongly urged that a new welcome center be built on the original site, which was near the Ohio River. Much of the opposition originated from tourism-dependent people in the lake counties who felt that a modern information center should be built with direct access to the interstate. These people contended that their opinions and concerns had not been considered during the decision making process.

In the months following the announcement, the issue was debated in a series of letters to the editor in the *Paducah Sun* The controversy came to a halt on December 10, 1981 during a three and one half hour public hearing on the project at Paducah's City Hall. Presiding over the hearing was Secretary Frank Metts. After listening to speakers on both sides of the issue, Secretary Metts stated, "This is not a McCracken County project and this is not a Marshall County project. This is a Kentucky project." He then thanked everyone for coming and reconfirmed his original decision to restore the Smith house.

Right: One of the upstairs bedrooms in 1981, with panes of glass and the mantel missing, trash scattered across the floor, and vines growing through the French doors. These doors lead to the wrought-iron balcony that overlooked the formal garden. Visible under the peeling wallpaper is the beautiful gray silk paper used in this bedroom suite by the Smith family.

PADUCAH, KY.   MONDAY, APRIL 12, 1982

The Paducah Sun

Edwin J. Paxton, Editor & Publisher 1900-1961
Edwin J. Paxton Jr., Editor 1961-1977

JACK PAXTON, Editor

FRED PAXTON, President

DON PEPPER, Editorial Writer

—Editorials—

Smith Mansion plan is attractive

The unveiling of plans for the restoration of the Smith Mansion here as a visitor center should allay at least some of the fears of our neighbors in the lakes area.

When the project was proposed, it raised a protest from people in the tourist business that it would not serve the purpose for which a visitor center had originally been planned. It was said that the project was mainly designed to benefit Paducah and McCracken County at the expense of the rest of the vacation area.

Now that the plans have been made public, it's apparent that what is being planned is not something less than the visitor center that the lakes area people wanted; it's much more.

The plans call for the two front parlors of the gracious antebellum house to be restored as museum rooms. The library will be a crafts and souvenir shop which could be an outlet for Kentucky-made products, and on the second floor a Jackson Purchase historical library

is planned.

The visitor information center, the original idea, will be housed in the downstairs dining room.

Thus the old house will serve not just the Paducah area; its focus is on the entire Western Kentucky region. It should be more effective, not less, as a lure for visitors to the lakes and vacation area.

That it will be possible to restore some of the grace and beauty which a 1907 remodeling brought to it, thanks to a set of interior photographs by David Barkley, is a bonus.

We are confident that when the restoration of the Smith Mansion, or Whitehaven, as we must get accustomed to calling it, is completed, sometime next year, it will prove to be a unique and compelling introductory attraction for visitors to our state and region.

The willingness of Transportation Secretary Frank Metts and Gov. John Y. Brown Jr. to persevere in support of this unusual project deserves commendation.

Restoration favored

EDITOR:

As the great-granddaughter of Edward L. Anderson, builder of the Anderson-Smith home on Lone Oak Road, I voice the need to restore this landmark.

In addition to the historic value, it was the home of my family for 43 years. Great-grandfather, a Paducah tobacconist, built the home during the Civil War and it was completed in 1866. The family of nine children and much company made a large home necessary. The family lived there 43 years. Within the walls, many eloquent and haunting stories of suffering, sharing, building and healing of the Anderson family before, during and after the war have emerged.

... ted the homeplace in 1975. ... January afternoon as I ... he porch to leave, I thought ... istory of our family, the ... hree trips there during ... , the sad love affair of ... . (Sam leaving home ... day never to return).

Aunt Irene dying of yellow fever, my mother as-a little girl playing dolls on the porch, Uncle John killing a man because he insulted the girl he was dancing with (this occurred at a neighbor's home.) Then ... the vision faded as bonds of kinship leaped across the years as echoes of their passing seemed to linger still.

Someone has said, "Daily, our ancestors are moving out of our lives, taking with them our heritage, not because they want to but because they think we don't care." Likewise, every day, this home is deteriorating before our eyes. The public is making an outcry for help. We are now begging for action. Please act now.

I, too, challenge the mayor of Paducah, John Penrod, to seriously look into this matter. Please contact the Society for Preservation of Paducah.

BONITA BURNLEY ABERNATHY
Box 63
Kevil, Ky.

Smith home has much

EDITOR:

For the past several years, there has been an increasing awareness of Paducah's rich history. This is evidenced by its citizens' concern to search for the history of and revitalize the downtown district and the surrounding older neighborhoods. Paducah is fortunate to still have buildings which are quite old, many of these in excellent condition.

The built environment is a record of how people in past times chose to live and interact with one another. One can look at the Market House and the Irvin Cobb Hotel to find examples of this.

For years the Market House w... an active center of trade, and w... very little imagination one ... picture how merchants lined ... building with their goods for t... open-air market. This building is... important reminder of how m... times have changed. In a sim... way, the Cobb Hotel, once the to... social center, is a record not onl... an architectural style, but of ... interaction of people of that time.

Just as these two structures ... the Smith House on Lone Oak R... and I-24 reflects on a society an... way of life which no longer exi... The mansion remains intact eno... to give one a perspective as to w...

Paducah can become more than 'just right'

EDITOR:

First, I lend a hardy amen to the letter from a former resident of Paducah in the May 22 issue of The Paducah Sun concerning the old Smith mansion on the Lone Oak Road. What a shame.

I am a resident of the city and have lived here my whole life and I hate to say that many of the changes I've seen in our town in my 32 years have been deplorable ones.

In my lifetime, I've had a... privilege of ...

than the smaller towns.

Paducah has a great deal of heritage to be proud of and to preserve. The only problem is that too much of that heritage has long since past.

I've seen many landmark buildings, the old city hall with its old clock steeple, Fire Station No. 1, the old Carnegie Library, the Kentucky and Rialto Theaters, the Oxford and Palmer House, the Oxford and ...

preservation of our history has been shown but again it seems to me as if even that, too, is terribly one-sided.

Evidently the only parts of the city anyone is concerned with preserving is eight or ten square blocks of the downtown area — and heaven only knows how the design of the new Convention Center complex will fit with the theme ...

My point though is mainly this: I feel many other people would try the same thing as us if our "city fathers" gave a little more attention and encouragement to the other parts of town as I believe that nearly everyone has heard enough of downtown for a while ...

Paxton's Support

As editor of the *Paducah Sun*, Jack Paxton was a constant force for civic improvement and historic preservation. His early and total support for the Whitehaven project provided much needed credibility.

In his editor's column entitled "Old Smith Place Struck a Chord," Jack correctly summed up that in proposing the project, community leaders had "put it to Frank Metts in a positive way and Metts pounced on the idea." Jack also recognized that the project had wide spread support. "The crumbling place has struck a chord. People from many walks, people from outside Paducah, people you'd least expect, talk about it." Jack correctly predicted the effect that this project would have on attitudes toward preservation by stating, "The saving of the Smith Mansion, as visible and remarked on as it is, as unlikely as the project once appeared, could cause a quantum jump in local attitudes toward preservation."

Below: Jack Paxton receives the Ida Lee Willis Award for Service to Preservation in 1983. This state award recognized his many contributions to the historic preservation cause, including support for the Whitehaven cause. Also pictured is Mrs. Paul Blazer.

Seeing the ultimate long term benefits, Jack wrote, "The effect will be cumulative, the effect on the way our town looks physically and upon the way we think of ourselves." Jack was certainly correct in recognizing the potential that the project had as a source of pride and distinction for our community and region.

o offer the community

rural life, though perhaps wealthier than most, was like to one family before the turn of the century.

On the grounds apart from the main house and in varying degrees of disrepair are a carriage house, underground cellar, cistern, and what appears to be quarters for servants. Walking through the grounds and in the living quarters, one can readily imagine this lifestyle where water must be drawn, electricity did not exist to light or cool, and transportation took place only by means of a horse or by walking.

It is quite distressing to see the deterioration that has occurred to this once-elegant landmark. Restoration would be difficult but certainly not impossible. Most problematic, as with many large and old buildings is what to do with them if restoration were to occur. What needs of the community could be met?

One possibility that might be investigated is the use of this building as the Kentucky-Paducah welcome center. Locating the center there could serve the community in three ways:
1. To provide a demonstration that Paducah is a progressive community proud of its heritage and optimistic of its future.
2. To advertise the many reasons to spend time in Kentucky and Paducah in particular. The economic benefit of the increased tourism alone might be reason to justify such a restoration.
3. To educate tourists and residents about the city's long history.

Though cost of restoration would be considerable for any future use of the building, many practical adaptations are possible if community support is shown.

MARK LARSON
2300 Harrison St.
Paducah

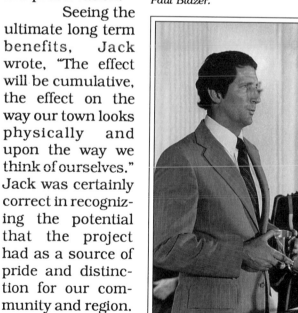

Archaeological Dig————————

A **set of fancy brass buttons that might have once** belonged to Edward Anderson, glass and clay marbles that once could have fallen out of a pocket of one of the Smith sons, a porcelain doll's foot that might have once belonged to one of Edward Atkins' two daughters, pieces of dishes broken by servants-- all of these long-hidden fragments of the past were uncovered at an archaeological dig that took place at Whitehaven in the early summer of 1982.

This exploration of Whitehaven's past came about because of the perseverance of Bill Black, Jr. and the interest of local and state officials. They recognized that the upcoming restoration and site preparation work could destroy the fragile archaeological environment of Whitehaven. In response to this concern, the Department of Transportation contracted with the Murray State University Archaeology Program and its staff archaeologist Kit Wesler to do a brief testing project at Whitehaven. The month-long project was a joint effort by the MSU archaeology program and the Jackson Purchase Archaeological Society.

The stated purpose of the project was to recover as much information as possible on the early occupation of Whitehaven. Kit Wesler, in his project report to the Department of Transportation, noted, "The value of this excavation lies not only in its new perspective on the history of Whitehaven, but also in its major contribution to a nascent historical archaeology of west Kentucky."

The project was impressive in its thoroughness. The first step in the project was to clear much of the dense brush surrounding Whitehaven, with much of the work done by hand. The area around the house was then staked out on a five by five meter grid, with postholes dug at each stake. The soil from each posthole was sorted and carefully bagged. In all, 192 postholes were dug, providing a thorough sample of soil and artifacts from the entire area surrounding Whitehaven.

The general finding from this posthole research was that artifacts tended to be found in the areas behind the main house, especially in the L-shaped area between the main house and the carriage house. This indicates a high traffic area, with lots of service activities going on. The lack of artifacts found in the front and west side of the house indicates that these areas were intended to be formal and more presentable to the public. Thus, they were either less used or better cleaned than the areas behind the house.

The posthole research indicated which areas should be more intensively investigated with excavation pits. Several of these pits, measuring 1.5 by 1.5 meters, were dug behind the house. From the postholes and the pits, over 15,000 specimens were uncovered and processed at the laboratory. The vast majority of the artifacts were brick fragments, pieces of coal, and iron nails. Other items uncovered included iron hinges, porcelain and wooden buttons, pieces of stoneware, brass beads, horseshoes, a stub-stem pipe bowl, an axe head, and a garter hook.

Above: A set of brass buttons, manufactured by the Benedict and Burnham Company of Waterbury, Connecticut in the 1840s, discovered in the archaeological dig at Whitehaven.

The most interesting artifacts discovered were a set of large, ornate brass buttons, each with an etched animal design on the face. These buttons were stamped on the back with the name Benedict and Burnham, a Connecticut firm that made these buttons in the 1840s. This date indicates that the buttons must have belonged to a member of the Anderson family, builders of Whitehaven in the 1860s.

Also discovered were one glass and several clay marbles. The baked clay marbles were probably made between 1884 and 1914, the glass marble between 1900 and 1926. It's easy to imagine one of the Smith sons dropping these marbles while playing in the back yard. Also found was a porcelain foot from a doll, which must have belonged to one of the Atkins' or Smiths' daughters.

In the future, additional research may be done with the artifacts found at Whitehaven. Through this

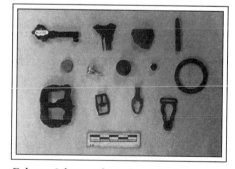

Below: Other artifacts found in the Whitehaven dig, including a key, hair comb, a doll's foot, marbles, and metal belt hinges.

Right: An excavation pit is dug at the rear of the house near the storm shelter. This pit proved to be the most productive one dug at Whitehaven.

Below: The same excavation pit almost completed, with the brick wall of the shelter exposed.

Below Right: One of the artifacts exposed in the dig, a brass lamp base, with pieces of glass nearby.

project, much valuable information about the historic past of Whitehaven was discovered and a major first step in the development of historical archaeology in the Jackson Purchase was taken.

Ground Breaking

Local and state officials and preservation supporters gathered in front of Whitehaven in June, 1982 to
witness the contract signing and ground breaking ceremonies. The past year had been spent planning the
project and getting the needed governmental approvals.
One behind-the-scenes effort involved Bill Black, Jr. and
myself in that we insisted that in all documents, the
house be referred to as Whitehaven, not the Smith
Mansion. We chose to resurrect the earlier, historic name
bestowed on the house when it was given in its Classical
Revival appearance in 1903.

Speaking at the ground-breaking cere-
mony, Secretary Frank Metts noted that the awarding of
a contract on the project just a year after the project was

*Above: Local supporters
and dignitaries join
Secretary of Transportation
Frank Metts for the ground-
breaking ceremony.*

*Right: Secretary Metts
addresses the crowd
gathered for the ceremony,
with the deteriorated
mansion looming in the
background, awaiting
restoration.*

born "established some credibility for government. We are doing what we said we would do." Secretary Metts revealed the importance of the project to the Brown administration when he said, "The State pushed it every step of the way. We prioritized it to make sure we accomplished what we intended to do." He revealed his own personal enthusiasm by stating, "I don't see how anybody can argue with it. We're saving a beautiful property that was about to go by the wayside for a heck of a lot less money than it would take us to build a new center."

Attending the ceremony were many of the local people who were valuable in pushing for and obtaining the project. This included the local elected officials, including Mayor John Penrod, Judge Raymond Schultz, Representative Dolly McNutt, and Senator Helen Garrett. Other local supporters attending were Growth, Inc. President Allan Rhodes and *Paducah Sun* Editor Jack Paxton. A key supporter and promoter of the project, Carroll Ladt, made the introductions to the crowd.

Part of the ceremony included the state signing a contract with the construction firm of Ray Black & Son for the restoration work on Whitehaven. The initial bid for doing this work was $720,740. In describing the upcoming project, contractor Bill Black, Jr. noted that the purpose was not to make Whitehaven a new home of an old home, but simply to make it like it was around 1907, but with modern electric plumbing, heating, and cooling additions.

Left: Secretary Metts signs the contract for restoration work with the president of Ray Black and Son, William R. Black, Sr.

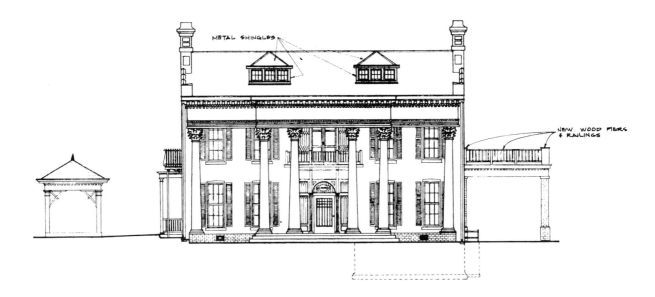

EAST ELEVATION

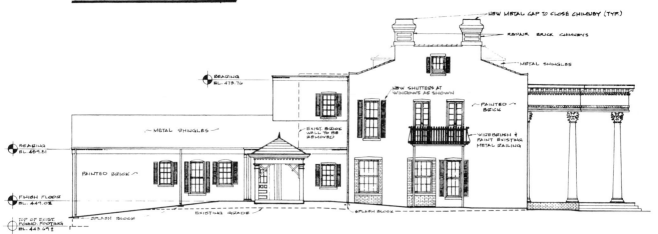

SOUTH ELEVATION

Building Elevation drawings by
J. Patrick Kerr, Architect . March 1982.

Early stabilization and demolition work includes (left) placing scaffolding under the front portico, (above) supporting the east wall with plywood and telephone poles, and (below) removing the rotted kitchen porch and roof and several rear rooms.

Restoration

After months of speculation and discussions, the state of Kentucky made an official commitment to restore the Smith House in the fall of 1981.

The first priority was to stabilize the house to prevent any further deterioration. The rapid decline of the house made it apparent that it would not survive the winter without immediate protection. The state appropriated $17,000 for the stabilization work, which was done by Ray Black and Son General Contractors with Marshall Fraser, their superintendent. Plywood and roofing felt were used to cover the roof to prevent any further water damage. The chimneys on the east side of the house were dismantled and the bricks carefully salvaged. Scaffolding was erected under the front portico to support it. Plywood was used to cover all the doors and windows of the house.

The area of greatest structural damage was the east wall of the house, which was collapsing into a pile of rubble. A huge hole had emerged where the library fireplace was located. This hole was enlarged when intruders knocked bricks out of place in order to climb through to gain access to the house. The wall was secured by covering it with sheets of plywood, then supporting these sheets with telephone poles.

Once propped up and secured, the house was able to survive the winter of 1981-82. One of our greatest concerns of this period was possible arson, especially in light of all the publicity and controversy surrounding the project. Almost every day, we would check to make sure the house was safe and secure. On several occasions, we had to climb through the attic windows onto the roof to resecure the roofing material. Other days, we walked around the house picking up pieces of architectural fabric that had fallen.

The winter of 1981-82 was a busy time, as

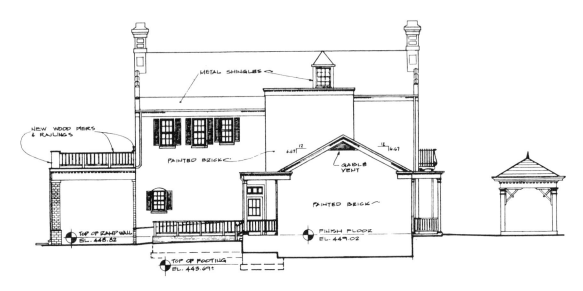

WEST ELEVATION

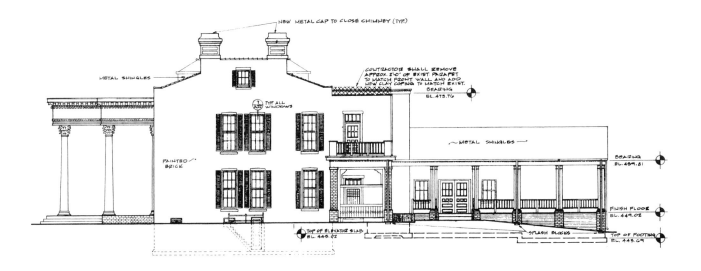

NORTH ELEVATION

Building Elevation drawings by
J. Patrick Kerr, Architect .   March 1982.

the planning for the restoration work took place. J. Patrick Kerr, of Paducah, was hired by the state to be the project architect. Pat has been an early advocate of the project and had assisted the state in obtaining the preliminary information needed to determine the feasibility of the project. Assisting Pat in planning the restoration and creating the architectural renderings were Richard Pair and Larry Sullenger.

Three basic decisions were made concerning the restoration work at Whitehaven The first was that, as much as possible, original building material would be salvaged and reused, instead of all new material being brought in and used. This meant that extraordinary efforts had to take place to identify, rescue, store and reuse original building artifacts. The second important decision was that Whitehaven would be restored to its 1903-1910 appearance. This meant that significant changes made by the Atkins and Smith families would be retained. The third basic decision was that, while the main house would be restored to its earlier appearance, the kitchen wing would be adapted to provide such functional aspects of a tourist welcome center as bathrooms, vending machines, and tourism pamphlets. It

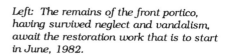

Left: The remains of the front portico, having survived neglect and vandalism, await the restoration work that is to start in June, 1982.

Below: Old KEEP OUT signs at the front door of the house were ignored for years by sightseers and vandals. In 1981, plywood was nailed over the first floor doors and windows to stop access into the house.

was this critical blend of historic restoration of the main house and adaptive use of the kitchen wing that made Whitehaven such an exciting and challenging project.

Another important factor in the restoration project was the selection of the right contractor to do the work. Being a state contract, the project was open to bidding by any qualified contractor. We all felt enormous relief when the low bid was submitted by the Paducah firm of Ray Black and Son. With such projects as the restoration of the old Peoples Bank Building, the Citizens Bank Building, and the Paducah Arts Council Building, this firm had exemplary credentials to do the restoration work at Whitehaven. Project contractor and dedicated preservationist Bill Black, Jr. had been an early propo-

Below: Project contractor Bill Black, Jr. shows off the light switches that he found for the house, an example of the exhaustive efforts he took to ensure a top-quality restoration job.

Above: The Ray Black and Son construction trailer stands in front of Whitehaven. Repair work has taken place on the front portico and east wall by this time.

Workers take down a wall in the upstairs bedroom, which would later be rebuilt with concrete blocks then replastered. The collapse of this wall was the major example of structural collapse on the interior.

nent of the project and his work on Whitehaven was a true labor of love.

An amazing team of regional craftsmen were gathered together to do specific parts of the restoration work. Ed Downs and Son, Inc., did the masonry work, which included rebuilding interior and exterior walls, reconstructing the elaborate fireplace in the library, and laying the brick sidewalks. The Paducah firm of Sawyer and Mathis provided the plaster work, which entailed replastering the walls and ceiling of the house, reproducing missing pieces of the decorative ceilings, and rebuilding the plaster capital of one of the front columns. This monumental task of placing together hundreds of pieces of the shattered capital was an extraordinary example of restoration work. The new mechanical systems, including new heating and cooling systems, were installed by Chester O'Donley. The new systems had to meet the demands of a public building without disturbing the historic fabric of the house. West Kentucky Sprinkler System installed a modern sprinkling system throughout the house, again without harming the historic character of the house. Jack Wallis of Murray reproduced all of the missing stained glass windows from photographs of the original windows. Industrial Sheet Metal installed the new shingle roof on the main house and a standing seam metal roof on the carriage house. A new electrical system was put into place by Beltline Electrics. The extensive mill work, which included reproducing missing woodwork, balusters, railings, and newel posts was completed by C.L. Triplett and the Owensboro Planing Mill. This

Restoration work begins on the kitchen wing. Work would include building a new brick wall and porch on the east side, but retaining the original brick walls on the west and north sides of the kitchen wing.

An extensive system of scaffolding and supports is erected around Whitehaven to secure it structurally during the restoration process.

Below: Wood supports are nailed onto the west wall of the kitchen wing to hold it up during the extensive demolition and reconstruction work on that section of the house.

Left: Scaffolding supports the front portico while restoration work takes place.

Because of extreme deterioration, a great deal of demolition work takes place in the kitchen wing.

Left: At the mid-point of the demolition work, the original concrete and tile floor is removed. Already gone is the roof and the butler's pantry.

Below: The same area later when all of the demolition work is finished. All of the flooring has been removed so that the extensive system of plumbing can be laid for the new bathrooms.

Right: A crane is brought in to assist with removing some of the rooms added to the rear of the house. This area is to be used for the new elevator and back upstairs hallway.

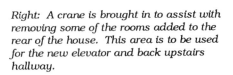

company also rebuilt the exterior wood column that supported the portico and that had collapsed into the front yard. The new brown and white tile floor and the tile map of Kentucky, both in the kitchen wing, were laid by the Cape Girardeau, Missouri firm named The Drury Company, whose hand tile setter was Frank Bursi. The painting of the inside and outside walls, which included scraping the loose paint from the woodwork, was by Shelby Painting Company of Paducah.

As the contractor and architect worked

Left: Construction on the kitchen wing includes building new decking for the roof and erecting a concrete block structure to contain the new elevator. An original wood lintel is reused on the new window for the upstairs area.

together to plan the restoration, extensive research was necessary to answer the many questions of how the house should be restored. Especially helpful were a collection of photographs of the Smith House taken in 1968 by David Barkley. These photographs provided a thorough documentation of the appearance of the house before it began to deteriorate. Specific questions about the earlier appearance of the house were answered by members of the Smith family, who took a great interest in the restoration work.

Before any restoration work took place, the

existing condition of the house was carefully documented, with photographs taken of each wall in each room of the house. These photographs were meant to provide a dramatic reminder of the original condition of the house.

As the restoration work progressed, periodic articles in the papers and television reports informed the public of the work achieved. This publicity also

DETAIL

FLOOR PLAN
J. PATRICK KERR 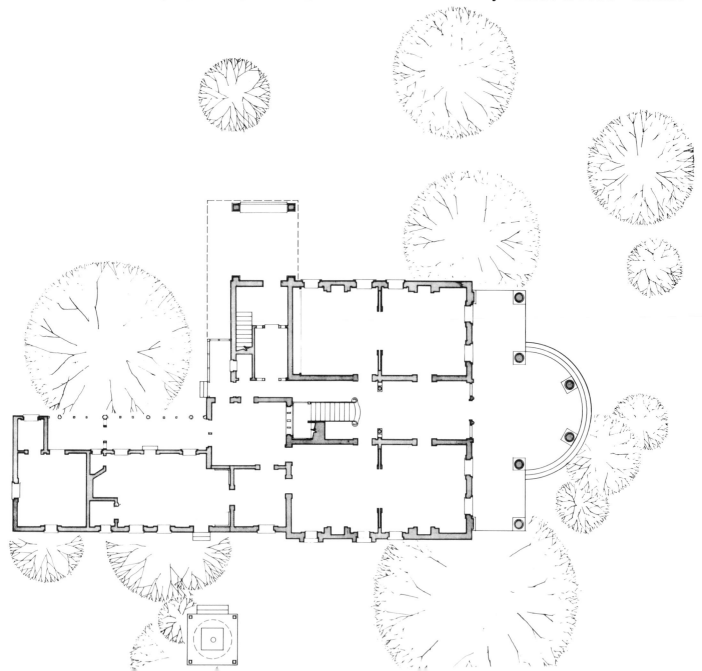 ARCHITECT AIA
126 SOUTH SECOND PADUCAH, KENTUCKY 42001

Above: Additional scaffolding allows workers to perform intricate restoration work on the front portico.

resulted in the return of many missing parts of the house, including light fixtures, hallway benches, library bookcase doors, the music room mantel, and the dining room's interior shutters.

The actual construction work began immediately after the contract with Ray Black and Son was signed in June, 1982. Each room had its own construction problems to be overcome. The condition of each room depended on the amount of water damage and vandalism. The first step in the restoration process was to clean out the house. It took about two weeks to remove all the garbage, fallen plaster, bed springs, tires, beer cans and loose lumber. Care had to be taken so that no significant pieces of architectural fabric were thrown out. Donnie Hunter and Floyd Wilson, laborers with Ray Birch and Son, handled much of this crucial, sensitive work.

HALLWAY

The condition of the front hallway was typical of most of the rooms at Whitehaven, with damage from water seepage and vandalism. Water damage was limited to the area around the main staircase. Vandalism damage was concentrated on the staircase and the pair of columns supporting the archway in the hall. Outlines on the walls indicated where the pair of hallway benches had once been. Restoration work on the hallway included putting a new coat of veneer plaster on all the walls, building a new column to replace the missing one, topping both hallway columns with new Ionic capitals, replacing the wood flooring around the staircase, and installing period glass in all the transoms above the doorways opening off the hallway. Because of the relative small amount of water damage in the hallway, the decorative plaster ceiling was in good shape and only small sections had to be replaced.

The character of the hallway was restored with the return of the pair of benches. These benches had

Above: Work on the hallway completed, with the floor refinished, the bench repainted, the column repaired, and the stenciling restored.

Left: The hallway before restoration, with the outline of the original bench visible. The remains of one of the hallway columns lays on the floor.

Above: Ray Black and Son Carpenters Jim Mitchell and Jack Taylor work old and new sections of the staircase handrail into place.

Right: A "before" view of the staircase, showing the vandalism damage to the handrail and balusters.

been installed by the Smith family during the refurbishing of the house by carpenters from Marshall Fields of Chicago. On these benches is where the Smith children would sit in the morning, waiting for their father to take them to school. The family also kept their family photograph albums in the storage area beneath the bench seats. The benches had been removed by someone who thought the house was going to be torn down. When he heard about the restoration, he graciously returned the benches. What is amazing is that the arms of the furniture still wore their original upholstery, dating back to around 1910. The benches were repainted and returned to their places of honor in the hallway.

Much of the hallway restoration work centered around the main staircase. This grand staircase had been installed as part of the 1903 remodeling. During the years when Whitehaven was vacant, vandals destroyed much of the staircase, including the balusters and handrail at the foot of the staircase. Water damage had weakened the support wall and landing so much that

The evolution of the restoration of the staircase.

Right below: The staircase at its worst condition, the victim of vandals who have stolen pieces of the bannister and spindles.

Right: A worker installs new spindles for the base of the staircase. A clamp holds a new section of the bannister in place.

Left below: The staircase after restoration.

it was precarious to go up the steps. The restoration work on the staircase was completed by general foreman Vernon Reynolds and carpenters Jack Taylor and Jim Mitchell of Ray Black and Son. The Owensboro Planing Mill manufactured 100 new balusters, new finials, the handrail, and the handrail's circular terminals. The old and new materials were combined so carefully that it is impossible to distinguish between them.

The existing treads of the staircase were in good shape and simply had to be cleaned and repainted. On the landing, a new wood flooring was put down by carpenters John Colvin and Marion Chaffin, who did most of the oak floor restoration. A new bearing stud wall was constructed to support the staircase. The area beneath the staircase, used by the Smiths as a coat closet, was also repaired.

Below: The simple elegance of the front hallway greets visitors to Whitehaven. The hallway exhibits such distinctive elements as stenciling, double built-in benches, a grand staircase, and an archway supported by Ionic columns.

Extensive work was required to replace the elegant, stately front door and side light windows. All that was left of the original front entrance was the wood frame for the side light windows and a small portion of the door. All of the original glass had been removed. Fortunately, the realtor for the Smith family, Joe Marshall, had photographs of all the original windows in the house. From these photographs, stained glass craftsman Jack Wallis from Murray, Kentucky, was able to reproduce all of the windows in the house. The front entrance is made of leaded bevel edge glass with stained glass insets in the sidelights. The only change made was to put the word "Whitehaven" in the glass above the door instead of the word "Bide-A-Wee." The change represented the new effort to call the house by its earlier historic name.

Right: Restoration work on one of the interior hallway columns includes repair of the column shaft and replacement on the Ionic capital.

Above: A close-up of the classical detailing of the archway in the hallway.

PARLOR

  Earlier in the restoration planning process, the front west room was designated the parlor. The parlor was the downstairs room with the greatest water damage. Water seepage had progressed through the roof, attic, and second floor to this room. In fact, it was possible to stand in one corner of the parlor and look up through the house and see blue sky. Because of the deterioration, much of the flooring and woodwork, especially on the west side of the room, had been destroyed.

  Restoration work on the parlor included replacing the floor joists and laying new flooring, replacing the baseboard on the west wall, scraping and painting

Although the room has suffered great water damage, much of the old woodwork in the parlor remains in good shape.

Above: Before any restoration work takes place, the southwest corner of the parlor bears great damage. From this corner of the room, it is possible to look up and see the sky through holes in the upper floors' ceilings and floorings.

the other woodwork, rebuilding the mantel, and laying a new fireplace hearth.

At one point in time, a modern ceiling had been installed in the parlor. During the restoration, the original ceiling height was returned and a new plaster cornice molding applied. This molding, called "Roman Ionic," was ordered from the Decorators Supply Corporation of Chicago. An elaborate ceiling medallion, called "Colonial" in the supply catalogue, was also ordered for this room and for the music room ceiling.

One exciting discovery was finding the original pocket doors between the parlor and dining room still nailed into place. Apparently these doors had not been used for years. The pocket doors between the library and music room were also in place. All of these were removed and reworked and returned to their tracks. The original brass hardware on these doors was missing, as it was on all of the doors in the house. The hardware for the pocket doors was replaced with original period pieces found in an architectural salvage shop in St. Louis. The chandelier in the parlor is also a replacement: a restored period piece found in an antique shop in St. Louis. By chance, the brass transom mechanisms in the parlor and the other rooms were still in place and still operational.

Whitehaven decorated for Christmas.

MUSIC ROOM

The room directly across the hallway from the parlor has always been called the music room by the members of the Smith family. The family kept a grand piano here and, along with the library, these rooms were the more formal areas of the house. The music room was

The music room has been decorated in subtle shades that compliment the floral stencil.

fortunate to escape major water damage while the house was vacant, and its floors, walls, and plaster ceilings were in comparably good condition. During the restoration process, the old layers of wallpaper had to be removed and the walls reveneered with a coat of plaster. After removal of the loose original plaster, all of the existing cornice molding was reused and new plaster was applied to wire lath attached to the existing ceiling joists.

The greatest discovery in the music room was found when paper was removed from the ceiling. Revealed was the outline of the original ceiling plaster decoration. The plasterwork, in the form of garlands and swags, had been applied in 1903 but later was removed and the ceiling repapered. The missing details were ordered from the Chicago Supply Company that produced the plasterwork in 1903 and was still producing the same decorations! The company spokesman said he believed this was the first time they had ever supplied materials to restore plasterwork which they originally made for a customer.

The mantel installed in the music room in 1903 is the most elaborate in the house. It has a pair of

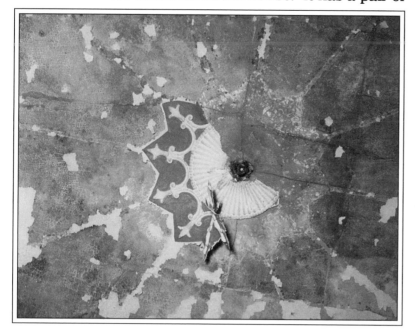

Left: A fragment of the ceiling medallion and the ghost of the original plaster decoration on the ceiling in the music room.

Above: Workers install the new plaster ceiling in the music room with details produced by the Chicago Supply Company, the supplier of the original ceiling in 1903.

Above: The music room mantel as it appeared in 1979, before it was stolen from the house.

Left: The reconstructed mantel, with the original upper portion reading WHITEHAVEN, lies on the floor of the music room before being put back into place.

fluted columns holding a swagged pediment with the words "Whitehaven" carved into it. During the Smith occupancy, a board covered these words because of the change in names. When the restoration began, all that remained of the fireplace were the white ceramic fireplace tiles and the outline of the mantel on the wall. We were able to find the original mantel pediment and return it to Whitehaven. The return of the mantel was an example of how hard we searched in an effort to restore Whitehaven to its earlier appearance with as much original material as possible. A pair of fluted columns and a glass mirror were added, matching the original parts of the mantel.

Not only did we recover the original mantel from the music room, we also found the original light fixture. One day a woman from Wickliffe, Kentucky, called me and said she had a light fixture from the Smith Mansion to return. From her description and by looking at David Barkley's photos, we knew that it was from the music room. When I drove to Wickliffe to pick it up, she told me that she bought the fixture at a flea market in Paducah to put into a new house that she was building. She decided to give it back so that she could bring her grandchildren to the house and show them what their family had contributed. She also admitted that she had done her own restoration work on it. A few of the prisms

were missing so she took apart a piece of costume jewelry and replaced the missing pieces.

The beauty of the music room was enhanced with the return of these missing pieces, including the mantel, the light fixture, the decorative ceiling, and the stenciling. The finished music room reveals the sensitive design talents of A. L. Lassiter, the architect of the 1903 remodeling. The graceful garlands of the plaster ceiling are repeated in the garlands of the stencil. The dogwood flowers carved in the swags of the mantel are repeated in the floral decoration of the stencil and also in the stained glass window over the staircase landing. The entire motif of the swags and finial of the music room mantel is also repeated in the stained glass window on the staircase landing.

Left: The restored music room mantel, with the original upper portion and new columns and capitals. Construction foreman Vernon Reynolds is reflected in the mirror.

Above: Restored and repainted, the music room mantel is the most beautiful in the house.

LIBRARY

Adjoining the music room is another room of great beauty, the library. This room has seen many changes to its appearance. When the house was constructed in 1860, the room had two back windows overlooking a rear porch. In 1903 the plaster ceilings and decorative fireplace were added to the room. Around 1910, these two back windows were enclosed when the Smith family added the rear staircase and entrance. This blank wall was covered by a five-sectioned bookcase. The beautiful doors of the bookcase were made of bevel edge glass. It was probably after the installation of this bookcase that the room was first used as a library.

As with the other rooms on the first floor, the most outstanding architectural feature of the library is the elaborate plaster ceiling. While the plasterwork in the music room seems very light and delicate, the library's ceiling has a heavier, more ornate feeling. Plaster ornaments with the faces of cupids highlight each corner of the ceiling. The middle of the ceiling is decorated with a large laurel encircling an elaborate central medallion. Running around the room is a wide band of bracketed cornice molding.

Right: The ornate plaster ceiling in the library, a combination of old and new pieces, has been installed but not yet painted.

Below: The old book shelves have the original bevelled glass doors that were removed from the house but returned as part of the restoration effort. Local citizens have donated the antique books for the shelves.

Above: A close-up of the beautiful plaster-work on the ceiling in the library.

Right: The library has been refurnished with comfortable reading chairs and a central library table, piled with books and accessories.

As with the music room, there was little water damage to the library during the period that the house was vacant. The greatest structural problem centered around the fireplace, where the exterior wall from the foundation to the roofline was collapsing. The yellow molded bricks from the fireplace fell in a pile into the room. Souvenir seekers took the decorative fireplace tiles and the marble shelves from the fireplace. When the doors and windows had been boarded up, curious people knocked out bricks in the fireplace to gain access to the house. The collapse of this wall also damaged the floor in the library and the plaster cornice molding above the fireplace.

When the restoration work began on the library, much of the surviving plaster decoration was removed and stored. The contractor found that the plaster segments were held in place by metal screws, which allowed easy removal. The plaster company of Sawyer and Mathis made new plaster casts of the details that had to be reproduced, including two of the cupid decorations. A third cupid was presented to Governor John Y. Brown at the dedication of Whitehaven. Sections of the cornice molding were made in Chicago, using as a pattern an original sent from the job. The large laurel surrounding the center medallion was ordered newly made from Chicago, but was patterned after outline marks found on the old ceiling.

Project craftsman Larry Mathis revealed that one of the hardest tasks was to try to find a piece of plaster that hadn't deteriorated too much so that a mold could be made. To recreate the cherub pieces, 30 coats of latex rubber were applied to one of the original cherub ornaments to create a mold. The new castings were made and put into place along with the surviving details. As a tribute to the excellent work of Mathis and his workers, it is now impossible to tell the new from the old.

Three sections of the original bookcase were also restored. We were excited to learn that when Elizabeth Smith Shelton moved out of the house in 1968, she took with her the bevel edge glass doors from the book-

Workers from the Sawyer and Mathis Plaster Company remove the central medallion from the library ceiling as part of the effort to salvage as much of the original decoration as possible.

case and had them installed as a window in her new house. We contacted Lourdes Hospital, the current owner of the house, who graciously donated the glass back to us. Doug Fiser, a local carpenter, rebuilt the bevel glass panels into the doors and installed them on the bookcase. In retrospect, we are very lucky that Mrs. Shelton took these doors with her. Otherwise, they would have been stolen or destroyed. The return of the bookcase doors is another example of original architectural fabric being brought back to Whitehaven.

Left: Masonry workers rebuild the brick fireplace in the library.

Right: Nine out of ten bricks in the finished fireplace in the library are the original ones salvaged at the beginning of the restoration process. Replacement bricks for the missing ones have been made with patching plaster.

Before and after the restoration of the fireplace in the library.

Left: Before restoration work takes place, plywood is used to cover the gaping hole in the fireplace. This is to prevent people from entering the house through this opening when the other doors and windows have been boarded up.

The largest structural problem that was dealt with in the library was the rebuilding of the fireplace. As the remnants of the fireplace were dismantled, all of the remaining bricks were carefully salvaged and laid out on the floor in the original configuration. About 90% of the original bricks were salvageable Only about two dozen new bricks had to be made with patching plaster to replace the missing bricks. The exterior wall

Below: The restored fireplace is testimony to the superb craftsmanship of brick mason Joe Ed Downs and his crew of workers.

Right top: The bricks for the fireplace are carefully laid out in sequence on the floor of the library before being put into place.

Right bottom: Brick mason Joe Ed Downs pauses at the mid-point of the work on rebuilding the fireplace.

Below: Reconstruction of the exterior east wall involved reconstruction of the wall with concrete blocks then veneering with the original bricks that had been carefully salvaged.

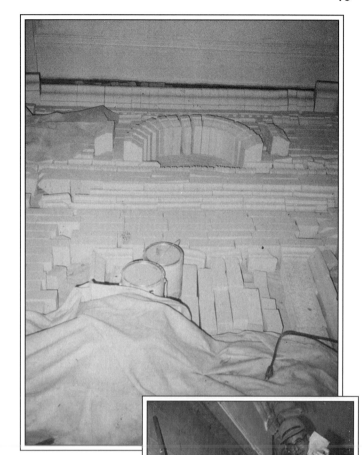

behind the fireplace was then rebuilt with concrete blocks. The fireplace was rebuilt with old and new bricks by Joe Ed Downs. The fireplace had been repainted a uniform yellow color prior to re-laying, thereby allowing the bricks to be distinguished from the mortar joints. One individual even returned a few of the missing fireplace tile, which made duplication of the other tiles possible.

Above: John Colvin, a worker with Ray Black and Son contractors, chips away peeling paint from a doorway in the library.

Right: The furnishing effort for the library has recreated a warm and comfortable room.

In examining the original fireplace, it was apparent that it had once held three marble shelves. At one time, someone had chipped away all of this marble. We did not know how to replace these shelves until Bill Black found a piece of the marble that the person had dropped. From this segment, Bill was able to determine the color, thickness, and shape of the original marble.

What may seem a small detail in the library actually reveals the amount of destructive energy that Whitehaven endured. One pane of glass in the transom over the door is the only original piece of glass in the house. Every other pane of glass in the house was broken by vandals. During the restoration process, we were able to obtain large sheets of old glass graciously donated by downtown Paducah merchants. This glass was from old windows that had been bricked up or from display cases. The old glass was then recut and used in the windows at Whitehaven. As a result, the waves and imperfections in this period glass contribute enormously to the atmosphere of the old house.

DINING ROOM

Connected to the parlor through the sliding pocket doors is the family dining room. The distinguishing architectural features of the dining room include the oversized windows that overlooked the formal gardens and the intricate plaster ceiling. The windows were probably installed by the Smiths around 1910 to provide a better view of the formal gardens being designed by Mrs. Smith. Wood louvered interior shutters run on tracks to block the strong afternoon sun. The large window sills provided an excellent place to set houseplants. The plaster ceiling in the dining room has a detailed vine motif. The cornice molding contains a raised pattern of grapevines and leaves, appropriate to the dining orientation of the room. Continuing this motif was the wall stencil, which also showed grapevines and grapes. The stencil pattern was found covered by layers of wallpaper, as was the outline of a plate railing that once ran around the room.

While the house was vacant, the dining room suffered tremendous damage due to water seepage, with about half of the ceiling falling to the floor. During the restoration process, scaffolding was placed under the ceiling and all of the surviving plaster pieces were salvaged and stored. New ceiling pieces were ordered from Chicago. Today, about half of the ceiling is original plaster and half is replacement, but it is impossible to discern between the old and the new.

The light fixture in the dining room was installed by the Smiths during the Marshall Fields redecoration of the house around 1910. The fixture has a ring of carved wood fruit painted in polychrome colors from which light globes hang. After being removed from the house after the Smith family left the house, the fixture was purchased at a local flea market by a resident of Lower Town. She purchased the fixture to convert into a mirror, but fortunately it sat on her back porch for several years, unharmed. We were able to repurchase it from her and return it to its original position in the dining room.

Above and below: Special efforts are made to remove and salvage portions of the plaster ceiling in the dining room.

It took special care to cut and install the large sheets of glass necessary to fill the two dining room windows. For several years after the restoration, the interior shutters were missing. Whitehaven Association Board member Bill Tullar found these in a warehouse where he stored antiques. They were among several items that he had purchased from the Smith family estate. Bill donated these back to Whitehaven and they were also returned to once again decorate and cover the windows.

Of special pride to Bill Black is the brass five-switch cover plate for the lights, a restored antique found after much searching.

Above: New plaster details that will be used to replace missing pieces of the dining room ceiling.

Right: The restored ceiling in the dining room.

Below: The restored dining room, with its intricate plaster ceiling and the original light fixture. The room now serves as the tourist information room.

SECOND FLOOR

Designed as private rooms for the family, the second floor is much simpler in decoration and architectural detail than the first floor. With its simpler design, the second floor was also less complicated to restore. Restoration efforts on these rooms centered on replastering walls and ceilings, replacing deteriorated flooring, reproducing the missing pocket doors in the two bedroom suites, and rebuilding the mantels and fireplaces.

The upstairs hallway is large enough to be a room. When the Smith family lived in the house, they

The restored upstairs hallway, looking toward the staircase.

furnished this area with comfortable chairs and sofas and used this as a sitting area. Mrs. Smith had a chaise lounge, which she loved to sit in while reading her cookbooks. The nicest feature of the upstairs hallway is the pair of French doors leading out to the second floor balcony which extends over the front entrance. The Smiths would often sit on this balcony in the evening. A pair of beautiful stained glass windows compliment these doors. The Smith family added the pair of mirrors in the hallway to provide more light. Restoration work on the upstairs hallway included rebuilding the double mirrors and the French doors and reproducing the stained glass windows, all of which was by Jack Wallis.

BEDROOM

The two bedroom suites open off the up-
stairs hallway. The bedroom suites are identical in size
and detail. The west bedrooms have French doors leading
to the wrought iron balcony that originally overlooked the
formal gardens. The rear bedroom also has a curved wall
closet, created when a staircase was built to the attic
area. This closet was always referred to as Mrs. Smith's

*Above: The rear upstairs hallway before
restoration. The stained glass window on
the staircase landing had been destroyed
by vandals.*

*Right: The staircase window after resto-
ration.*

closet.

       Several rooms on the second floor, including two bathrooms, a rear bedroom, and a sun porch, were removed at the beginning of the restoration process. The area where the rear bedroom was located, behind the stained glass windows of the staircase landing, was used for the new elevator which was installed. Another bathroom and dressing room area, originally located off the east bedrooms, was restored as an office for the

Above: The upstairs hallway and staircase window before restoration. Right: Stained glass artist Jack Wallis installing the new staircase window.

Left top: The restored mirrors in the upstairs hallway reflect each other endlessly.

Opposite page above: The stained glass windows in the upstairs hallway are exact reproductions of the original ones.
Opposite page below: Upstairs hallway decorated for Christmas.

Below: Light streams through the beautiful windows and door in the front hallway. The hall tree has been decorated for Christmas.

Whitehaven staff. The adjoining room over the carport, used by the Smiths as a sun porch then as a bedroom, was removed and made into an outdoor sitting area.

THIRD FLOOR

With six active children, Mr. and Mrs. Smith must have discovered early the need for additional play space. In response to this need, they converted the third floor attic space into a playroom for the children. All of the walls of the playroom were decorated with fanciful murals of Oriental scenes, including pagodas, willow trees, and exotic animals. Two front dormer windows were added to provide light and alcoves for activities. Windows were also added to both gable ends of the third floor. Elizabeth Smith Shelton remembered that before the windows were put into place, a square piano was hoisted on a crane and moved into the third floor. The third floor also had shelves for storing toys and games. The two Smith daughters had a small cast-iron stove in

Above: Wonderful scenes of fruit trees, pagodas, and willow trees decorate the walls of the attic area, once used as a playroom for the Smith family children. Top right: Before restoration work begins, the north wall of the master bedroom suite had collapsed. The wall will be rebuilt with concrete blocks to provide structural strength and the doorway to the bathroom removed.

Below: The restored master bedroom suite.

which they could build fires and cook. The smoke was vented through a pipe outside. On Christmas Day, the children would walk up the steps to the play area and each find a Christmas tree, lighted with real candles. One of the Smith's grandsons set up an elaborate train set in the play area. Years later, a box of electric train tracks was found in the carriage house. The square piano remained on the third floor until the 1970s, when it was dismantled and moved. It is now housed in a home in New Orleans.

Because of its limited access, the attic has never been open to the public. Most of the heating and cooling equipment for the second floor was installed in this area. This space is also used for storage. All of the wall stencils, however, were kept exactly as they were.

Curved wall accentuates the bedroom closet that was created when the staircase was built by the Smith family to the attic play area. This pre-restoration photograph also shows one of the iron hot water radiators laying on the floor.

Below: Exotic scenes of tropical dens are drawn on the walls of the attic area. These scenes were done when the Smiths converted the attic into a playroom for their six children. The attic is now used for storage and to hold heating and cooling equipment.

Above: The original pocket doors between the two rooms in the master bedroom suite are missing.

Left: New pocket doors for the master bedroom suite are reproduced based on the sliding doors that survived on the first floor. These doors had been nailed into position and not discovered by vandals.

The beautiful front portico of Whitehaven before and after extensive restoration work has taken place.

EXTERIOR RESTORATION

The philosophy for restoring the exterior of Whitehaven was the same as for restoring the interior. As much original architectural fabric as possible would be salvaged and reused. Missing pieces for the building would be duplicated so that the original appearance, circa 1903-1910, would be returned. As with the interior, a dedicated team of workers and craftsmen performed outstanding work on the exterior restoration effort.

As the outside restoration work began, the two most visible and immediate needs were the rebuilding of the front portico and the reconstruction of the collapsing east wall. Each of these monumental tasks was accomplished with great sensitivity by the team of workers.

The front portico of Whitehaven is the single most important and recognizable architectural feature of the house. It was the addition of this portico in 1903 that transformed Whitehaven from a farmhouse to a mansion.

Left: Despite considerable damage to the exterior of the front portico, the ceiling of the porch and the capitals of the columns remain in good shape before restoration work begins.

Below: The long pole descending from the ceiling of the porch once held the fan that provided the breeze for summer evening get togethers.

After years of neglect, the portico was an abused relic of its former glory. Water deterioration had rotted huge sections of it. Almost every day it seemed, it was possible to go out to the house and find pieces of the front portico that had fallen into the yard. The severe deterioration of the front portico was proven the day that one of the front columns collapsed into the front yard and shattered into pieces.

As the restoration work began, the immediate concern was to stabilize the front portico so that no more deterioration took place. Once stabilization took

Below left: During the period of decline, the west column collapsed into the front yard. The remnants of the column and its plaster capital were carefully salvaged for restoration later.

Below right: The wooden shaft of the column has been repaired by the Owensboro Planing Mill.

place, it became obvious that some of the architectural features of the portico were still in good shape and could be salvaged. Remaining intact were five out of the six Corinthian columns, part of the cypress decking, the ceiling, and the concrete steps leading up to the portico. Needing restoration work were the plaster cornice molding, the column bases, the woodwork of the five foot architrave, and sections of the cypress decking. A major

Left: A worker installs new cypress decking for the floor of the front portico.

Below: The flooring of the front portico is a combination of old and new decking.

area of concern was the rebuilding of the column that had fallen into the yard.

Work on the portico began quickly. The original flooring of the portico was one and one half inch thick cypress. The central portion of the flooring, out of reach of weather and water damage, was still in good shape and was reused. Damaged floor joists and decking on the outer part of the portico were removed and replaced by identical cypress components.

The wood bases to the columns were severely deteriorated and almost all of these had to be rebuilt. New concrete block supports were constructed under each column base, to provide enduring stability for future years. The existing columns and plaster capitals were patched and repaired as needed.

Several of the holes in the columns that had to be patched were caused by bees. For years, one of the front columns had been home to thousands of bees. Smith family members remember honey dripping out of this column and down the front steps. Bees also lived in the walls of the house, and at one time, honey dripped down the wall in the music room! Despite many efforts, the bees manage to return to the portico at Whitehaven each year.

Right: A close-up of the plaster detailing on the entablature of the front portico before restoration.

Below: The restored upper portion of the front portico at Whitehaven.

The most visible signs of water deterioration on the front portico were concentrated on the architrave of the projecting half-circle of the portico. The original portico had a flat roof and built in gutters. Over the years, as the gutters were neglected and allowed to fill up with debris, water accumulated and rotted away the wood guttering system. The water damage then spread to the wood cornice and the plaster eaves.

During restoration efforts, a new roof and metal guttering and flashing system were installed. Because of severe deterioration, about half of the plaster eave consoles and dentil molding had to be removed and replaced with new plaster reproductions.

Intensive efforts were necessary to restore the fallen column, which had shattered into pieces. After finding the column in the front yard, Bill Black and I picked up the wood staves of the column shaft and stored

Above: The west column of the front portico, which once lay in pieces in the yard, now stands back in position after restoration.

Left: A special clamp invented by Bill Black, Jr. allows one of the portico columns to be held in place while the column base is rebuilt.

these inside the house. We also picked up the hundreds of plaster pieces that had been the Corinthian capital. During the restoration, the wood staves were sent to the Owensboro Planing Mill, which glued the pieces back into the original shape of the column.

Restoring the plaster capital was a more monumental task. While it would have been easier to simply make or buy a new capital, we wanted to rebuild the original capital, if possible. Bill Black, Jr. and the craftsmen of Sawyer and Mathis Plaster Company took the hundreds of pieces and glued them back together, just like a giant jigsaw puzzle. A few of the missing pieces

Below left and right: Workers return the reconstructed plaster capital to its former position atop the west column. The many pieces of the shattered capital were put back together like a giant jigsaw puzzle. The rebuilt column was carried to the top of the scaffolding, sawed into halves then placed back into position.

had to be remade by Sawyer and Mathis, both by casting and sculpting. After being reinforced, the restored capital weighed almost 400 pounds. The capital was hoisted to the top of the scaffolding, cut in half, and remounted in its original position. Today, this reconstructed capital is visually identical to the others.

EAST WALL

The other area with enormous structural damage was the east wall, which was collapsing in one section from the foundation to the roof line. The area of deterioration was concentrated along the chimney running from the library to the upstairs bedroom to the roof. This wall area was stabilized with sheets of plywood supported by telephone poles. During the restoration, workers had to take down by hand the entire section of wall. The dismantled bricks were carefully salvaged and stored. The new wall of concrete blocks was built, then reveneered with the original salvaged bricks. The craftsmanship of the bricklayers was so fine that it is now impossible to discern the area of the wall that had to be rebuilt.

Considerable demolition work was required on the east side and rear of the house. The bedroom that had been built over the carport was removed, with the dentil molding salvaged for reuse on other parts of the house. Also removed were the sun room and porches added by the Smiths to the rear of the house.

Right: Masonry workers veneer the east wall with the original bricks that had been carefully salvaged when the wall was dismantled. A new wall was built of concrete blocks to provide structural strength before the brick veneer was added.

Bottom right: Combining old with new, a new east wall has been tied into the original north wall. Also being built is a new two-story addition to hold the elevator and its mechanism.

Bottom left: The old and new brick walls have been painted white and a new side porch added. This delightful side porch is one of the most successful elements of design at Whitehaven.

Four stages in the restoration of the exterior of the kitchen wing.

Above: The east porch of the kitchen wing, before restoration, has suffered considerable deterioration.

Above right: During the demolition period, the roof of the kitchen wing is removed, along with the rear bathrooms and porches on the main house. Considerable demolition work is necessary to prepare the kitchen wing for new bathrooms and elevator to be installed.

KITCHEN WING

The kitchen wing required partial demolition as it was to be adapted to serve the functional part of the new welcome center. The entire wing was gutted so that the plumbing for the bathrooms could be installed. The areas that had once been the breakfast room and butler's pantry were also gutted. These areas now provide space for the elevator shaft and a closet for the maintenance staff. The original west and north walls of the kitchen wing were retained, but a completely new east wall and side porch had to be built. A brown and white glazed ceramic tile floor, one almost identical to the original floor, was laid by the Drury Tile Company of Cape Girardeau, Missouri. As a special attraction of the new welcome center, a blue and white tile mural was laid showing the state of Kentucky, with each county outlined in black tiles. A special red tile proudly marks Paducah. A pleasing feature of the kitchen wing is the new side porch. Furnished with old-fashioned rocking chairs, this porch has become a favorite spot for travelers to stop and rest.

Above: The kitchen in 1980, with only the old cook stove still in place.
Below left: Workers from the Drury Tile Company lay the new tile floor in the kitchen. The brown and white tile floor is a close replica of the original floor.
Below: Where the butler's pantry once stood, a new tile floor showing the Commonwealth of Kentucky has been laid. The counties of Kentucky are shown in University of Kentucky Wildcat blue, but McCracken County is marked with a red tile.

Some of the finishing touches at Whitehaven.

Left: A new brick wall has been erected welcoming visitors to the Whitehaven Tourist Welcome Center and the Commonwealth of Kentucky.

Left below: Workers put up new shutters on the front windows. These shutters were based on the two original shutters left on the house.

Above; Splash blocks for the downspouts were made from large blocks of limestone donated by Coy Stacey. Here Don Wilson creates a hollow in one of the stones with a sandblaster.

OTHER EXTERIOR WORK

More restoration work that took place on the exterior of Whitehaven involved installing a new metal shingle roof and painting it dark green, building new shutters for the windows, replacing the wood decking on the wrought iron balcony off of the master bedrooms, building a new railing and balusters for the front balcony, and covering the exterior heating and cooling units with latticework.

C. L. Triplett, owner of the Owensboro Planing Mill, displays some of the new newell posts made for the bannister for the front balcony. Some of the new doors for Whitehaven remain on the truck behind him.

One night of anxiety took place when the new metal shingle roof was painted. The primer color for the roof was an incredibly ugly color of mustard yellow, which had to dry for 24 hours before the final color could be applied. I personally answered 12 telephone calls of complaints from people thinking that this was the permanent color. The next day the roof was painted dark green.

OUTBUILDINGS

Restoration efforts were extended to the two outbuildings on the grounds--the gazebo and the carriage house. The gazebo was constructed to cover the cistern, where the family's supply of drinking water was stored. At one time, an intricate system of guttering covered the house and channeled the water into this cistern. The

Left: One of the important features restored on the grounds at Whitehaven is the gazebo, which was built over the cistern that stored drinking water.

Below: The restored gazebo provides a comfortable place for visitors to Whitehaven to sit and enjoy the beauty of the house.

water passed through a charcoal system located near the back kitchen door. The gazebo also provided a sitting area near the formal gardens. Before restoration, the gazebo was in good shape, except for leaning slightly. The base of each square column had to be rebuilt and the gazebo was repainted white. The original metal roof was retained and painted green to match the main house's roof. Benches were added and each spring hanging baskets of flowers and ferns are put out.

The west side of Whitehaven greets most visitors to the tourist welcome center.

The original restoration plans called for the demolition of the carriage house, which was in terrible shape. The roof had collapsed and vegetation completely covered the building. We recognized the historical importance of this building and the contribution it made to the setting at Whitehaven. We also knew that it could provide storage area for the maintenance staff for lawn mowers and tools. Bill Black personally lobbied Frank Metts, who arranged for the carriage house to be included in the restoration effort. The exterior brick was repainted white, with dark green used to highlight the doors, windows, and roof.

Today it is hard to imagine the Whitehaven complex without the carriage house. It serves as a headquarters for the staff in providing a workshop area, office, and break room. The staff has built on a greenhouse, as a place to winter plants to start seedlings. Besides its functional role, the carriage house serves as

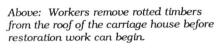

Above: Workers remove rotted timbers from the roof of the carriage house before restoration work can begin.

Right: The carriage house before restoration, with the collapsed roof and overgrowth of vegetation.

Left: The restored carriage house meets many needs for the welcome center, including providing space for an office, employee lounge, workshop, storage area, and greenhouse.

a reminder of the network of outbuildings once needed to service a mansion like Whitehaven.

The only other surviving outbuilding is the storm shelter built by Mr. Smith in the 1940s. Now part of the grounds, it also serves as a storage area.

BRICK SIDEWALKS

The first restoration plans called for concrete walks leading up to Whitehaven. We felt this would not be appropriate to a historic house. Bill Black convinced the Department of Transportation to change the work order so that all of the sidewalks around Whitehaven would be laid with old sidewalk bricks from Paducah. Many of these bricks, dating back to the turn-of-the-century, had been salvaged by the local preservation society during street projects in the downtown area. Other bricks came from local brick supplier Len Lockwood, who had been saving them for himself but was willing to part with them for this special project. Twenty seven thousand bricks were needed for the sidewalks, of which nine thousand were discarded because they were not worn enough.

From years of use, the bricks had a smooth, walked-on surface that could never be duplicated in modern bricks. The new sidewalks were laid in a running bond pattern that copied remnants of three old brick sidewalks found on the site during restoration. The bricks were laid on a dry mortar mix that had been spread on top of a concrete base. After an entire section was laid, the dry mortar was sprinkled with water so that the bricks were set into place. By this method, no mortar was used between the bricks, preventing future deterioration and cracking.

All of the brick sidewalks were laid by Ed Downs and Son Brick Contractors, under the direction of Joe Ed Downs. The craftsmanship of this firm was impeccable. In an article on Whitehaven in the *Paducah Sun*, Mr. Downs revealed, "Restoration work is tough. It's

Above and right: Workers install sidewalks made of antique paving bricks in front of Whitehaven. The bricks are being laid on a concrete foundation on top of a layer of dry mortar. After the bricks are laid, the dry mortar is soaked to bond the bricks to the concrete.

one of the most trying jobs you can get, but we call ourselves professional, so everything has to be perfect." In the restoration effort each brick used in building the sidewalks was examined to make sure that the worn surface was left exposed.

Finishing touches on the grounds included creating a picnic area for tourists, complete with tables and grills, installing period lighting along the sidewalks, returning an antique fan to suspend from the ceiling of the front portico, and placing light fixtures on the two front columns of the portico.

Workers shovel gravel along the concrete foundation of the sidewalk to provide drainage.

Much more work was completed on the grounds around Whitehaven by the Harper Construction Company. Grading the site, building the access road leading to and from Whitehaven, and paving the parking lots for the cars and trucks to stop at the welcome center were necessary. The total bill for this work was around $2 million.

SUMMARY

The restoration process on Whitehaven took only nine months of the allotted one year to complete. Each day, it was exciting to go out and see what had been accomplished. Recognizing the importance of this project, we took over 2000 slides during this time.

I think that the most exciting day in the restoration period was when the house was first re-painted with a fresh coat of white paint. It took that coat of fresh white paint to really prove to me that the house was going to be saved and restored. It was also a signal to the world of what was going on at Whitehaven. I remember watching drivers going by on Lone Oak Road, weaving across traffic lanes, trying to see the newly painted house. It was quite a sight!

By June of 1983, the restoration process at Whitehaven was complete and the house was ready to open to the public. Several factors combined to make the restoration of Whitehaven a fascinating and fulfilling

project. The open approach by state officials, the sensitive design by the architect and his staff, the fantastic attention to detail and thorough commitment by the contractor, the incredible craftsmanship of all the workers involved—all of these forces combined together to make the restoration of Whitehaven a source of pride and distinction.

Stenciling

While the house was at its worst state of deterioration, it seemed to reveal some of the secrets to its history and development. One of these was the discovery of stenciling on the interior walls of Whitehaven, hidden for decades under layers of wallpaper. This type of stenciling was a common decorative feature in American homes at the turn-of-the-century. It was an especially favorite decorative device of architect A. L. Lassiter, who apparently chose the stencil for Whitehaven after the 1903 remodeling. He also used stencils in his design of the Carnegie Library and the Frank Fisher house.

The stencils at Whitehaven are a combination of geometric patterns and floral designs. The basic design for each stencil was painted in an oil-based medium in sepia tones, with color washes added to provide color and depth. The front hallway had a very formal stencil of garlands with a square border. The parlor had two layers of stencils. The bottom layer was a wide pattern of consecutive circles crossed by a larger feather. A later stencil painted over this was comprised of a block pattern painted in greens and purples. The stencil in the dining room had the appropriate motif of grapes and grape vines, matching the grapevines in-

scribed in the eaves of the plaster ceiling. In the music room, a stencil of garlands entwines with dogwood blossoms and leaves. This stencil complimented the garlands of the plaster ceiling and the dogwood blossoms carved into the mantle. No stencils appeared in the library, apparently because the elaborate plaster ceiling did not

Above: During the summer of 1981, Ann Brown led a group of volunteers who spent two weeks at Whitehaven recording the patterns of the original stencils. Here Ann records the blue ribbon stencil that was on the walls of the east bedroom suite.

need additional decoration. Upstairs, the north bedrooms had the most elaborate stencil in the house, a repeated blue ribbon pattern on which birds and flowers had been painted by freehand. Apparently, this room was originally decorated for Ed Atkin's two daughters. Stencils were also found in several of the back hallways and in the upstairs hallway.

After this wealth of stencils was discovered, it was apparent that steps would have to be taken to record these before the restoration work began. During the restoration period, all the interior walls would be repaired and covered with a fresh coat of plaster. The need to record these stencils was discussed by Bill Black, Pat Kerr, and myself on a public access television show on the Whitehaven project. Responding to this concern was local craftsman, Ann Brown, who organized a volunteer group who spent two weeks in the deteriorated house recording each stencil pattern. The effort took place while the house was in its most deteriorated condition, with plaster falling from the ceiling and giant holes in the floor. Because all of the windows were boarded up, light was provided by connecting a series of extension cords from a utility pole in the yard. Access was gained to the house by climbing through one of the broken front windows in the music room.

Ann Brown and her dedicated group of volunteers traced the stencils directly onto clear plastic,

which was later used to make a pattern on heavier paper. The copying process was complicated in some cases when the pattern, and the wall it was on, would crumble when touched. The stencils in the parlor were especially difficult to copy because of the rotting floors and walls. In this room, I gingerly climbed a ladder and quickly copied the pattern. I also photographed each stencil in the house, so that the original paint colors could be copied. We found one stencil, though, in the downstairs back hallway, in mint condition because it had been covered with a mirror for seventy years.

One of the top priorities of the Whitehaven Association, Inc. in its furnishings effort was to restore the original stencils to the walls at Whitehaven. Ann Brown was hired by the association to stencil the walls in the front hallway, the parlor, and the music room. Eighty years after first being applied, the stencils at Whitehaven were returned in their fresh, glowing colors. The exquisite craftsmanship of Ann Brown was remarkable, especially under the trying working conditions she endured. Much of her work was executed while perched on precarious scaffolding and under the view of crowds of tourists visiting Whitehaven.

Another talented local craftsman, Ginia Manchester, continued the effort in January 1988 with her work to restore the stencil in the upstairs hallway. Ginia painted the ribbon and heart stencil pattern in brown then shaded in areas of green, red and yellow. A special challenge was working on scaffolding constructed over the staircase area that allowed access to the top of the walls.

The stenciling shines as one of the decorative highlights at Whitehaven— one that is constantly marvelled at and admired by the visitors to the mansion.

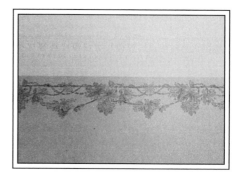

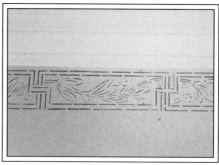

Top: The restored stencil in the music room features flowers and garlands. The stencil coordinates with the garland effect of the ceiling and the flowers carved into the mantel.

Above middle: The basic pattern along the baseboard in the music room has been stenciled on the wall. Ann Brown later hand colors the stencil with red and green.

Among the dignitaries present at the Grand Opening Ceremonies were Governor John Y. Brown, Jr. and former Secretary of Transportation, Frank Metts. Secretary Metts is prepared to perform the official ribbon-cutting.

Grand Opening

On the hot summer afternoon of June 23, 1983, the long-awaited grand opening ceremony for the Whitehaven Tourist Welcome Center took place. An excited crowd of over 2500 people joined Governor John Y. Brown and his cabinet for the ceremony. For all of us who had worked on the house, it was like unwrapping a present for the public.

For the Whitehaven Association, Inc. Board of Directors, assisting the state in planning the ceremony was their first important project. Preparations consisted of mailing out thousands of invitations, inviting special guests to the ceremony, training guides for tours of the house, and finishing last minute work on the house. In lieu of any furniture being in the house, large photo-

The official letterhead art is designed by artist Garry Redmon.

Kentucky Transportation Secretary Frank Metts at the Grand Opening ceremony.

graphs were hung on the walls showing the interior before restoration. In the hallway, historic photographs of the house were hung. These photographs were paid for by a gift from Sigma Epsilon International, a sorority that was interested in the project. Large ferns were hung from the front balcony, in remembrance of the hanging baskets which Mrs. Smith always placed on the front porch.

The ceremony included the presentation of colors by the Fort Campbell Color Guard, a blessing of the house by Reverend Tim Taylor, and comments by Governor Brown, Secretary Frank Metts, and Whitehaven Association President Dolly McNutt.

In his comments, Governor Brown gave credit to Secretary Metts for motivating the state into restoring the mansion and substituting it for a "plastic" rest stop. Recognizing that the project was an important achievement, Brown stated, "You have something here that you can be proud of for another 130 years. What you

WHITEHAVEN

DEDICATION
June 23, 1983

Call to Attention
Carroll Ladt
Master of Ceremonies

Invocation
the Rev. Timus Taylor
Grace Episcopal Church

National Anthem and Raising of the Flag
John Drew and the Fort Campbell Army Band
and Color Detail

Welcome and Introduction of Platform Guests

Remarks by James Runke
Secretary of Transportation

Remarks by Frank Metts
Former Secretary of Transportation

Remarks by Governor John Y. Brown Jr.

Ribbon-cutting Ceremony

My Old Kentucky Home
John Drew and the Fort Campbell Army Band

Presentation of Gifts
Representative Dolly McNutt

Our thanks to the Council of Garden Clubs of Paducah
for providing the flower arrangements and to
Epsilon Sigma Alpha International for providing
the photographs displayed in Whitehaven.

have accomplished here is you have restored a piece of history that will serve us well and teach us for years to come."

Secretary Metts noted that the house had died from disrepair, but had not been buried yet. The house was brought back to life by workmanship that he described as "astounding." Dolly McNutt added that Whitehaven would serve two masters— tourism and preservation.

Immediately following the ceremony, hundreds of people toured the house for the first time. Thousands of others watched the ceremony on a live broadcast from Whitehaven by WPSD-TV.

Whitehaven Association, Inc._____

Realizing the need for local involvement in the Whitehaven project, Secretary of Commerce Bruce Lunsford and Governor John Y. Brown appointed a board comprised of citizens from the region to serve as a volunteer advisory group for the development of Whitehaven. This group met for the first time in March, 1983 and formed the Whitehaven Association, Inc.

The first task of the Whitehaven Association Board of Directors was to plan the grand opening ceremony. The Board worked with the state and made the necessary local arrangements. A corps of volunteer tour guides was trained to provide tours of the house immediately after the ceremony.

After the grand opening, the next task facing the Whitehaven Association was to initiate the furnishings and decorating of the house. State officials informed the association that state funds would not be available for this. Realizing that the furnishings effort would take several years, the association decided to print large posters showing views of each room in the house before restoration work took place. These posters vividly provided the visitors to Whitehaven an impression of "before" and "after".

A furnishings subcommittee was set up to supervise the decorating of Whitehaven. The committee was dedicated to ensuring that the decorating and furnishing of the house would be appropriate to the 1900-1910 Classical Revival period. A brochure on the furnishings needs at Whitehaven was prepared with the assistance of Image Graphics and mailed to potential donors.

The public response to the furnishings needs at Whitehaven has been tremendous. Each proposed donation to Whitehaven has been reviewed and voted on according to appropriateness and need.

Noting the need for funds to assist in the furnishings effort, the Whitehaven Association has sponsored a variety of fund-raising events. Special functions at Whitehaven have been a Victorian Christmas tea with an old-fashioned St. Nicholas, an evening cocktail buffet party, and springtime candlelight tours of the house and gardens. The association also sells packets of stationery with the Whitehaven logo on each card.

The association members make a special effort each year to decorate the house for Christmas. Local garden clubs work with the association in setting up Christmas trees for each of the rooms downstairs. A large tree is also installed in the upstairs hallway. The mantels, tables, and hall tree are decorated with candlesticks and poinsettias. Holly and evergreen wreaths are hung on the front balcony and on the windows. The festive celebration of Christmas makes Whitehaven an extra-special stop for all visitors.

The Whitehaven Association continues its efforts to improve and enhance the welcome center. A dedicated Board of Directors meets monthly to plan activities that will assist in the development of Whitehaven. The public is invited to become members of the Whitehaven Association. Their tax-deductible membership dues provide much needed funding for the projects of the Whitehaven Association.

Furnishings

The primary responsibility of the Whitehaven Association has been to furnish and decorate the rooms at Whitehaven. A team of dedicated volunteers has worked together to furnish Whitehaven in an attractive and authentic manner. The primary goal has been to return Whitehaven to its former glory as a grand mansion, full of elegant items and furniture appropriate to the 1903 period. The furnishings effort has depended on the generosity of local citizens to donate the items and funds necessary for this effort. Many local supporters have donated beautiful antiques from their homes so that they can be enjoyed by the visitors to Whitehaven. Other people have supported the fund raising projects of the Whitehaven Association so that furnishings could be purchased. This community- wide effort has resulted in an elegant enhancement of the mansion.

HALLWAY

The visitor to the historic part of Whitehaven first enters the entrance hallway. Dominating the hallway is an elaborate Renaissance Revival hall tree, donated by Mrs. Chapman Jennings. It originally came from her family's home in Henderson, Kentucky. Nestled by the staircase is a handsome grandfather's clock, donated by Mr. and Mrs. Burt Throgmorton.

Adding a feeling of elegance to the hallway is a pastel of Empress Eugenie, donated by Anne Washington Leslie and her family. This pastel and a matching one in the parlor were brought to Paducah from New Orleans by Mrs. Leslie's grandfather in the 1850s. The pastels were by the school of Franz Winterhalter, the European court painter. They hung in the Washington family home on Broadway for over ninety years before being donated to Whitehaven in May, 1988. They are among the most valuable items donated to Whitehaven.

The only other decorative touches in the hallway are the pair of benches and the stenciling. Future furnishings for the hallway could include an oriental rug for the floor, a runner for the staircase, and various old fashioned hats, coats, and parasols for the hall tree, especially those that would revive the memory of the six Smith children who once lived in the house.

PARLOR

The decorating philosophy behind refurnishing the parlor has been to make it the most elegant room in the house; one appropriate for special occasions and guests. The formal tone of the room is set by the beautiful stenciling running beneath the cornice molding. Resting in the middle of the room is a large Empire sofa, covered in a soft green damask. This piece, along

Above: The parlor has been decorated with pieces of elegant furniture appropriate to a mansion like Whitehaven.

Right: An elegant writing desk, such as one which would have been used by the lady of the house for her correspondence.

Left: The huge square piano dominates the music room. Other antique musical instruments add to the atmosphere of the room.

Below: The bevelled glass front door is reflected in the mirror of the hall tree in the front hallway.

with several other pieces in the house, is on loan to
Whitehaven from the Office of Historic Properties in
Frankfort, the state agency responsible for maintaining
Kentucky's state-owned historic sites. The sofa and other
pieces of furniture were sent to Whitehaven in 1983 by
former First Lady Phyllis George Brown, who was interested in assisting with the furnishings effort.

Standing between the two front windows is
a tall Eastlake pier mirror. After this mirror was purchased by the Whitehaven Association, it was discovered
that it originally came from the Sinnott Hotel at Second
and Broadway in downtown Paducah, a building once
owned by James P. Smith. The beautiful gold and green

*Above left: The tall pier mirror between the
two front windows in the parlor once stood
in the Sinnott Hotel in downtown Paducah.*

*Left: The sofa in the parlor is on loan to
Whitehaven from the Office of Historic
Properties in Frankfort. Other pieces of
furniture have been donated by local
citizens or purchased by the Whitehaven
Association.*

draperies in the parlor windows were made from material donated by Dr. and Mrs. Louis Myre. The brass hardware for the draperies in the parlor and the music room was donated by Mr. and Mrs. Pat Parrish.

Other pieces in the room are a pair of Rococo Revival side chairs donated by Mr. and Mrs. Chris Gould and a mahogany card table donated by Dr. and Mrs. Ted Borodofsky. Pieces purchased by the Whitehaven Association are an inlaid writing desk and a mirrored petticoat table that once graced a Natchez mansion. The funds to purchase these items and several others were donated by the Paducah Tourist Commission. Several Meissen figurines, given by Mr. and Mrs. Ralph Young, help decorate the room as accessories along with a brass banquet lamp, given by Mr. and Mrs. Robert Wenzel from the Wheeler family estate. Future decorative touches for the parlor may be lace curtains in the windows, and additional accessories, such as china figurines or a stereoscope.

DINING ROOM

Early in the restoration process, the state designated the former dining room as the site for the tourist information room. Operated by the state Department of Tourism, this room provides space for the tourism staff to dispense travel information and to welcome visitors. Serving as a desk for the staff is a massive former grocery counter, found by architect Pat Kerr in Bardwell, Kentucky.

In the fall of 1986, the Department of Tourism redecorated the room by painting the walls in a warm shade of terra cotta and setting up an exhibit of Kentucky crafts. Featuring such items as Shaker boxes, quilts, and Berea textiles, the exhibit introduces visitors to the beauty and quality of Kentucky crafts. On the walls of the room are photographs of Kentucky tourism sites such as Churchill Downs and Kentucky Lake, by James Archaumbeault, a Kentucky artist. In the future, the Whitehaven Association hopes to restore the grapevine motif stencil to the walls of this room.

MUSIC ROOM

The decorating of the music room has allowed the Whitehaven Association to collect and display several interesting musical instruments. Dominating the room is the large square piano, which was manufactured by the W. K. Kimball Company of Chicago around 1870. This piano once traveled up and down the Ohio River on a riverboat and later was used in a saloon in Metropolis, Illinois. The piano was donated to Whitehaven by the Denney family of Sturgis. Other musical instruments featured are an antique violin, accordion, and zither. The most unusual instrument in the room is a pianola, manufactured by the Aeolian Company of New York in 1904. This instrument was pushed up to the keyboard of a piano and pumped while a roll of music was inserted. It would then play the piano for you. It was donated by Mr. E. C. Gray.

Above: A graceful gentleman's chair stands in the corner of the music room.

Above: The square piano in the music room once travelled on the Ohio River on a riverboat and later stood in a Metropolis saloon.

Left: An unusual musical instrument, the pianola, will automatically play the piano with the insertion of a music roll and the pumping of the pedals.

Completing the music room atmosphere is a needlepoint piano stool, donated by Mrs. Henry Whitlow in memory of her mother, Florence Clement, and an inlaid music cabinet donated by Beverly Johnson. Other significant pieces of furniture in the room include an early twentieth century Mahal rug donated by Dr. and Mrs. Rob Robertson, a pair of balloon back side chairs donated by Dr. and Mrs. Walker Turner, a fireplace bench donated by Dr. and Mrs. Gary McMillan, and a gentleman's chair covered in needlepoint donated by Mr. and Mrs. Andrew Lampkin. Two lithographs, each showing scenes of French music rooms, were purchased by the Whitehaven Association. The elaborate lamp on the piano was donated by Mrs. Louis Igert, III. Future acquisitions for the music room could include a period harp and additional paintings for the wall, especially watercolors matching the floral stenciling in the room.

Below: Sheets of old music rest on the piano, part of the re-creation of the music room atmosphere. One sheet of music is appropriately "My Old Kentucky Home".

Left: Old books and pieces of china are displayed on the center table in the library.

LIBRARY

The library has been furnished as a comfortable room in which family members could gather to read, to talk, or to smoke. Standing by the fireplace is a large gentleman's smoking chair, donated by the Nagel family from the living quarters of the Nagel and Meyer Store in downtown Paducah. Within close range is a mahogany smoking stand with a drawer for storing tobacco and pipes, donated by Marjorie Wood.

Positioned in the middle of the room is a square library table, covered with period books, a lamp, and pieces of china. Standing against the wall is a large Empire buffet, on loan from the Office of Historic Properties after being donated to the state by a Frankfort family. Hanging above this buffet is one of Whitehaven's most valuable possessions, "The County Election" by G. E. Bingham. This monochrome painting was donated to Whitehaven by the descendants of Charles Wheeler, a prominent Paducah lawyer and U. S. Congressman.

Contributing to the atmosphere of the li-

Below: The comfortable reading chair in the library was donated by the Nagel family of Paducah.

brary is the collection of period books on the shelves of the bookcase. These books have been donated by dozens of local citizens and range in scope from family Bibles to children's adventure books to the classics, typical of the reading tastes of any family. The muted colors of the books behind the bevelled glass doors create a mellow atmosphere for the library.

Other pieces of furniture in the room consist of an upholstered library chair donated by Dr. and Mrs. James Metcalf, a marble-topped table and lady's rocking chair donated by Dr. and Mrs. Gary McMillan, an old gas lamp decorated with painted moose heads donated by Mrs. Tom Threlkeld, and a silver epergne with milk glass insert donated by Mrs. B. H. Van Antwerp.

Future plans for enhancing the library involve covering the walls with a period wallpaper, laying an oriental or bear skin rug on the floor, and installing shutters on the windows.

UPSTAIRS HALLWAY

The upstairs hallway is usually empty of furniture to allow large groups of visitors in this space. Possible future furnishings may be a table and rug for the center of the hallway and chairs, a chaise lounge, and sofa for the area near the French doors. The stenciling in the hallway and above the staircase was restored in 1988 by Ginia Manchester.

BEDROOM SUITE

The west upstairs rooms are being developed as an elegant bedroom suite, appropriate to the owners of such a grand house. The front room has been made into a sitting room, with various chairs and couches. The back room holds a large Renaissance Revival bed, covered in a hand crocheted coverlet. Other items in the rooms are a Victorian fainting couch given by Mr. and Mrs. James Brockenborough, a walnut wash stand and chest of drawers given by Dr. and Mrs. Gary

Left: The massive wardrobe in the upstairs bedroom suite takes the place of a closet.
Above: A Victorian fainting couch folds out to make a day bed.

Opposite page: A family Bible is one of the books that is displayed in the library.

McMillan, a cherry rocking chair given by Mrs. Robert Wenzel, a tuxedo couch given by Mrs. Fred Burch of Frankfort, a set of china bedroom accessories given by Mrs. Tom Threlkeld, and a walnut wardrobe donated by Mr. and Mrs. Ray Krosp and a pair of Victorian chairs by Mrs. L.E. Albritton and Mrs. Paul Feldsien.

An extensive effort has been made to add accessories to provide a cozy atmosphere to the bedroom suite. Among the small items that have been donated are a family Bible by Mr. and Mrs. J.O. Sumner, a three-piece dresser set by Mrs. B.H. Van Antwerp, a Victorian lamp by Mrs. William Blalock, a walnut case clock by Mr. and Mrs. Paul Jett, and a family photograph by Mollie Morgan. Various pieces of antique clothing and accessories have been given for display in the bedroom, including an 1860 dressing gown by Joy Lamon, a 1920s wedding dress by Mrs. Clyde Love, ladies white kid slippers by Mrs. Ed Michael, satin shoe trees by Mrs. Harry Livingston, opera length white gloves by Eleanor Coffman, a ladies' petticoat and beaded bag by Marianna Ringo, a white satin wedding dress and wedding shoes by Hanks Batts, and a pair of spectacles by Mrs. James Rieke.

Covering the floors in the rooms are a pair of Oriental rugs, donated by Dr. and Mrs. Steve Clymer. These rugs were the first items donated to the Whitehaven furnishings effort and remain the most valuable possessions in the house. They came from the historic mansion Oaklands in Murfreesboro, Tennessee. Hanging in the windows of all the upstairs rooms are lace curtains purchased by the Whitehaven Association.

Future additions to the bedroom suite should include a period wallcovering, possibly a gray silk wallpaper similar to the one applied by the Smiths, damask swags over the windows, and additional accessories that would have been found in a bedroom of the period. Of all the rooms at Whitehaven, the bedroom suite should be the coziest and least formal.

Below: The large Victorian bed dominates the upstairs bedroom. This piece is one that was purchased by the Whitehaven Association.

Barkley Rooms

The Alben Barkley rooms were opened at White-haven in the summer of 1984. These rooms contain historic memorabilia purchased at the auction of the Alben Barkley estate, located in Paducah, in June, 1984. All of the items were purchased with funds raised in the "Save Angles" campaign to preserve Alben Barkley's home as a historic site. Growth, Inc. also developed and donated to Whitehaven a photographic exhibit illustrating Alben Barkley's life and career.

Above; Historic items in the Alben Barkley rooms include his portrait, his collections of walking canes and shaving mugs from the U. S. Senate Barber Shop, and his desk and chair.

Among the items purchased at the auction and now on display at Whitehaven:

The teakwood desk and chair presented to Vice-President Alben Barkley by the President of the Phillipines;

The roll-top desk used by Barkley while he served as a U.S. Congressman in Washington;

The first Vice-Presidential flag, designed by the Department of the Army by order of President Harry Truman;

Barkley's collection of walking canes, senatorial shaving mugs, gavels, and keys to the city;

The tuxedo, top hat, and Bible used at Barkley's inauguration as Vice-President in 1948;

A portrait of Alben Barkley that hung above the mantel in the library of Angles, his Paducah, Kentucky home.

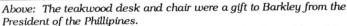

Above: The teakwood desk and chair were a gift to Barkley from the President of the Phillipines.
Top right: Barkley had this magnifier made so that he could read his speeches without wearing his glasses.
Right: The rolltop desk was used by Barkley while he was a U. S. Congressman.

The majority of the $50,000 raised from the "Save Angles" campaign went to purchase the memorabilia. The remaining money was used to set up the photographic exhibit on Barkley's life and career. These photographs, taken from the Barkley family scrapbooks, show Barkley in the roles of U.S. Senator, Majority Leader of the Senate, keynote speaker at the Democratic National Convention, Vice-Presidential candidate, and Vice-President of the United States. Other photographs show him at home at Angles and on the campaign trail. This exhibit was developed to educate visitors to the Barkley rooms on the local, state, and national significance of Alben Barkley's life.

Large photographs illustrate Alben Barkley's life and the rise of his career from local lawyer to Vice-President of the United States.

Memorial Garden

While the Smiths lived at Bide-A-Wee, the grounds west of the main house were extensively developed as formal gardens. Here Mrs. Smith would gather flowers for the house or to be taken down to the First Presbyterian Church.

The memory of these formal gardens was revived when the Marian Widener Memorial Garden was added to the grounds at Whitehaven. The garden was named in honor of Marian Widener, an original member

of the Whitehaven Association, Inc. Board of Directors and one of the most beloved citizens of Paducah. Marian was largely responsible for the landscaping scheme at Whitehaven, working closely with the Department of Transportation and Sanders Nursery when the grounds were landscaped in 1983. In fact, Marian completely altered the original landscaping plan, substituting dogwoods, azaleas, boxwoods, and hollies for the originally proposed plantings.

The lovely cutting garden at Whitehaven provides color from early spring to late fall.

After Marian's death in 1985, the Whitehaven Association, Inc. decided to plant a cutting garden on the grounds of Whitehaven and name it in her honor. Donations from friends and admirers paid for the plantings and site work. Mrs. J. William Young and Mrs. Richard C. Smith planned the garden, designed to provide blooms from spring until fall. In the spring, groups of tulips, jonquils, crocuses, and irises bloom. During the summer months, there are marigolds, coreopsis, Michaelmas daisies, zinnias, and phlox.

A sidewalk paved with historic Paducah paving bricks surrounds the entire garden. On one side, a white Chippendale bench provides a spot for visitors to sit and admire the garden.

Standing at the end of the central vista of the garden is a lead statue of a wood nymph. The piece of English statuary from Charleston, South Carolina was found by members of the garden committee. Funds to purchase the statue were donated by Marian Widener's three children. White dogwood trees have been planted behind the statue. Other iron benches on the grounds at Whitehaven were donated by Mrs. Marion Bichon and Miss Emily Schroeder, and Mrs. Richard Smith.

Publicity

A project as exciting and innovative as the Whitehaven restoration was bound to attract state and national attention. The project has been covered in several national publications. *Southern Living* magazine published a one-page spread on Whitehaven in the April, 1985 issue. The article described the efforts to save the house and explained its current use as a tourist welcome center. Black and white photographs accompanying the article showed the Alben Barkley memorabilia and the side entrance.

The winter, 1987 issue of *Victorian Homes* magazine also featured Whitehaven in an article prepared by Lexington writer Marty Godbey. The six page article included ten color photographs taken by Marty and her husband Frank Godbey. The article focused on the craftsmen who worked on the restoration. Those quoted included Bill Black, Jr., project contractor; Larry Mathis, head plasterer; Ann Brown, stencil artist; Jack Wallis, stained glass maker; and myself.

A color photograph of Whitehaven appeared on the cover of the January, 1985 issue of *Back Home in Kentucky* magazine. Illustrating an article entitled, "Our Kentucky Homes", Whitehaven was described as "representative of the best among Kentucky's many historic homes." One of the highest honors awarded Whitehaven was inclusion in the book, *Remaking America*, by Barbaralee Diamonstein. This book, focusing on the most exciting adaptive use projects in America, is considered one of the most important publications of the decade concerning historic buildings. Forty eight projects from across the country were selected from the thousands submitted for inclusion. Whitehaven is only one of two projects chosen from Kentucky—the other being the Carroll County Jail, which was restored for a museum and offices.

I submitted Whitehaven for inclusion in the book after reading about the project in *Preservation News*. I mailed before and after photographs and a description of the history and restoration of Whitehaven. Several months of correspondence resulted between the author's office and myself. The inclusion of Whitehaven in this book recognizes its innovative use of a historic house and the superb quality of the restoration.

In describing the projects found in *Remaking America,*, the book's jacket states that Whitehaven, "a once-splendid Civil War-era mansion in Paducah, long neglected, now welcomes visitors to Kentucky." National attention was focused on the publication of this book. Barbaralee Diamonstein was interviewed on the Today Show by Jane Pauley. An article on the book was included in *USA Today*. The book was reviewed in *Insight Magazine*, a publication of the Washington Post, which also included a photograph of the front of Whitehaven being painted. The Smithsonian Institute has prepared an exhibit of photographs and text from this book, which is currently travelling the country. We hope to bring this exhibit to Paducah some day.

On the local and state levels, Whitehaven has become a symbol for progress and pride. A photograph of Whitehaven was included in a special Kentucky advertising section in the January 30, 1986 issue of *USA Today*. Whitehaven has also been featured in the "Oh, Kentucky" advertising campaign conducted by the state Department of Tourism. Recent brochures by the Paducah Chamber of Commerce and the Paducah Tourist Commission also prominently display Whitehaven. Even the local television station uses a beautiful shot of Whitehaven in its station identification spot.

Several newspapers have featured Whitehaven in articles. In March, 1986, Associated Press writer Joyce A. Venezia interviewed Mrs. Richard Smith and me. The resulting article on the historic and restoration of Whitehaven was printed in newspapers all across Kentucky, including Louisville, Lexington, Winchester, Bowling Green, and Owensboro. The article was accompanied by a photograph of Mrs. Smith and myself admiring the mantel in the music room.

Some Final Words

Surrounded by busy roads on all sides, Whitehaven stands as an island of beauty and heritage in a very hectic world. As a tourist welcome center, Whitehaven now serves its greatest purpose. Instead of providing a place to live for one family, it yields shelter and comfort to thousands of people. The positive response to Whitehaven by these people has been extraordinary. Some time in May of 1988, the 1,000,000th person stopped at Whitehaven since its opening as a tourist welcome center. I'm sure that most of these people have realized that they were visiting the most beautiful and unique welcome center in America.

The restoration of Whitehaven has had a significant impact on our community. The effort to save Whitehaven illustrates the positive accomplishments that can be made when everyone bands together and works for a common good. The restoration of Whitehaven has also taught us two important lessons in historic preservation. First, no matter how deteriorated, it is never too late to save and restore a truly important building. Second, this region is blessed with workers and craftsmen who can perform outstanding restoration work.

My own continuing involvement in the Whitehaven project has brought me joy and inspiration. It is always a pleasure to run out to Whitehaven, whether it is to take some photographs or to give a house tour to a class of third graders from a local school. One of my greatest pleasures is to go through the Whitehaven guest book and read the warm and appreciative comments by visitors. These range from "Great restoration" and "Friendly staff" to simply "Wonderful" and "Fantastic". It's always nice to know that our efforts are appreciated.

Richard Holland

RICHARD HOLLAND
September 29, 1988

WHITEHAVEN: REBIRTH OF A SOUTHERN MANSION
Mail to:
McClanahan Publishing House, Inc.
P.O. Box 100
Kuttawa, Kentucky 42055

TO ORDER CALL TOLL FREE
1-800-544-6959
Visa & MasterCard accepted

Please send me _________copies of

WHITEHAVEN: REBIRTH OF A SOUTHERN MANSION	**@ $21.95 each**__________
Postage and Handling	**@ $2.00 each**__________
Kentucky residents add 5% sales tax	**@ $1.10 each**__________
TOTAL	__________

Make check payable to McClanahan Publishing House

Ship to:
Name____

Address______________________________________

City____________________State__________Zip__________

WHITEHAVEN: REBIRTH OF A SOUTHERN MANSION
Mail to:
McClanahan Publishing House, Inc.
P.O. Box 100
Kuttawa, Kentucky 42055

TO ORDER CALL TOLL FREE
1-800-544-6959
Visa & MasterCard accepted

Please send me _________copies of

WHITEHAVEN: REBIRTH OF A SOUTHERN MANSION	**@ $21.95 each**__________
Postage and Handling	**@ $2.00 each**__________
Kentucky residents add 5% sales tax	**@ $1.10 each**__________
TOTAL	__________

Make check payable to McClanahan Publishing House

Ship to:
Name____

Address______________________________________

City____________________State__________Zip__________